Mortido

Angela Betzien

Currency Press, Sydney

CURRENT THEATRE SERIES

First published in 2015
by Currency Press Pty Ltd,
PO Box 2287, Strawberry Hills, NSW, 2012, Australia
enquiries@currency.com.au
www.currency.com.au
in association with Belvoir, Sydney

Copyright: *Mortido* © Angela Betzien, 2015.

COPYING FOR EDUCATIONAL PURPOSES
The Australian *Copyright Act 1968* (Act) allows a maximum of one chapter or 10% of this book, whichever is the greater, to be copied by any educational institution for its educational purposes provided that that educational institution (or the body that administers it) has given a remuneration notice to Copyright Agency Limited (CAL) under the Act.
For details of the CAL licence for educational institutions contact CAL, Level 15 / 233 Castlereagh Street, Sydney, NSW, 2000; tel: within Australia 1800 066 844 toll free; outside Australia 61 2 9394 7600; fax: 61 2 9394 7601; email: info@copyright.com.au

COPYING FOR OTHER PURPOSES
Except as permitted under the Act, for example a fair dealing for the purposes of study, research, criticism or review, no part of this book may be reproduced, stored in a retrieval system, or transmitted in any form or by any means without prior written permission. All enquiries should be made to the publisher at the address above.

Any performance or public reading of *Mortido* is forbidden unless a licence has been received from the author or the author's agent. The purchase of this book in no way gives the purchaser the right to perform the play in public, whether by means of a staged production or a reading. All applications for public performance should be addressed to The Yellow Agency, PO Box 736, Surry Hills NSW 2010, Australia; ph: +612 8090 421; email: contact@theyellowagency.com

Cataloguing-in-publication data for this title is available from the National Library of Australia website: www.nla.gov.au

Typeset by Dean Nottle for Currency Press.
Cover image: Colin Friels by Julian Meagher.
Cover design by Alphabet Studio.

Contents

MORTIDO

    Act One   1

    Act Two   31

    Act Three   46

    Act Four   80

Theatre Program at the end of the playtext

Currency Press acknowledges the Traditional Owners of the Country on which we live and work. We pay our respects to all Aboriginal and Torres Strait Islander Elders, past and present.

ACKNOWLEDGEMENTS

Leticia Cáceres, Ralph Myers, Anthea Williams, Eamon Flack, Jean Mostyn, Justine Goss, Karen Colston, Lizzie Cater, Sarah Louden and The Yellow Agency, Tim Roseman, Peter Matheson, Colin Friels, Tom Conroy, David Valencia, Renato Musolino, Louisa Mignone, Luke McGettigan, Rachel Chant, Sean Proude, Geoff Cobham, Andrew Howard, Robert Cousins, Pete Goodwin, Kurt Luthy, Otis Jai Dhanji, Calin Diamon, Toby Challenor, Mathew Goldwyn, Geordie Brookman, Blazey Best, Kate Mulvany, Gary Brun, Lily Newbury-Freeman, Dan Wyllie, Nathaniel Dean, Marshall Napier, Pete Goodwin, Jody Betzien, Sibylle Kaczorek, Eri Brody, Sebastian Bourges, Rodolfo Guerrero, Helen Weder, Sonja Elliot, Mat Ward, Jodie Le Vesconte, Scott Witt, Belvoir and State Theatre Company of South Australia staff.

Special thanks to Playwriting Australia syndicate: Joanna Davidson & Julian Leeser, Laura Golis, Amy Merriman, Andrew & Louise Sharpe, Peter Wilson and James Emmett.

Angela Betzien

Mortido was co-commissioned by Belvoir and Playwriting Australia.

Playwriting Australia seeks, develops and champions new Australian stories for the stage. We exist to ensure there are more astonishing new plays on the Australian stage; to make certain that those plays are as extraordinary as possible; and to ensure that the range of writers creating these plays is as wide as possible, reflecting the Australia we live in. We actively seek out unrepresented voices, especially Indigenous and culturally and linguistically diverse artists, to address the imbalance in Australian theatre. We are the only national organisation working with playwrights and theatre artists from all backgrounds and at all levels of their careers. We connect talent with opportunity to extend the art of playwriting and advocate for positive change on behalf of artists, industry and audiences.

This play was also supported by a grant from The Literature Board of The Australia Council.

*In memory of Maria Josefina Capello.
To Brianna, for her faith and resilience.*

Mortido was first produced by Belvoir and State Theatre Company of South Australia at the Dunstan Playhouse, Adelaide, on 20 October 2015, and Belvoir St Theatre, Sydney, on 11 November 2015, with the following cast:

OLIVER / ALVARO	Toby Challenor & Otis Jai Dhanji (Sydney); Calin Diamond & Matt Goldwyn (Adelaide)
JIMMY	Tom Conroy
DETECTIVE GRUBBE / OTHERS	Colin Friels
SCARLET / SYBILLE	Louisa Mignone
MONTE / DARREN SHINE	Renato Musolino
EL GALLITO	David Valencia

Director, Leticia Cáceres
Set & Costume Designer, Robert Cousins
Lighting Designer, Geoff Cobham
Composer, THE SWEATS
Sound Designer, Nate Edmondson
Dramaturg, Anthea Williams
Movement Director, Scott Witt
Assistant Director, Rachel Chant
Dialect Coach, Jennifer White
Stage Manager, Luke McGettigan
Assistant Stage Manager, Sean Proude

Mortido is a co-commission with Playwriting Australia.

CHARACTERS

DETECTIVE GRUBBE, mid 60s
JIMMY, mid 20s
SCARLET, early 30s
MONTE, late 30s
OLIVER, Scarlet and Monte's child, 7
EL GALLITO, 20s
SYBILLE, Berliner, early 30s
HEINRICH BARBIE, German Bolivian, mid 60s
ALVARO, Bolivian boy, 7
CHRISTOS LYMBIOUS, Greek Australian, 50s
BRATISLAV ACKERVIK, Serbian Australian, mid 60s
DARREN SHINE, late 30s

The play can be performed with a cast of six, assuming the following distribution of roles and doubling:

GRUBBE / BARBIE / CHRISTOS / BRATISLAV
JIMMY
SCARLET / SYBILLE
OLIVER / ALVARO
EL GALLITO
MONTE / DARREN

SETTING

The design should be fluid enough to conjure a range of locations.

All characters and events appearing in this work are fictitious. Any resemblance to real persons, living or dead, is purely coincidental.

This play went to press before the end of rehearsals and may differ from the play as performed.

ACT ONE

GRUBBE: Once there was a boy born in the *barrios* of Chilpansingo, Mexico. Now the Boy's Mother was poor. Her husband was a good-for-nothing drunkard who beat his wife. Fortunately he died when he fell off the back of a *cempasùchil* truck after drinking too much *mescal* on an empty stomach. Everyone said The Boy's Mother was better off without that lazy *chuntara* and although The Mother wept for him, she had her son and he was a blessing and all a mother could pray to Our Lady of Guadalupe for. Without her husband, The Mother did not have enough *tortilla*. She went to all the *maquiladoras* begging for work but there was none.

So, The Boy said to his Mother:

Madre, let me go into the city to work and bring home some pesos so that you and I can eat.

The Mother sighed.

My child, you are only seven. What would you do?

I can shine shoes, Madre.

Very well.

For she knew that without pesos they would surely starve.

The next day The Boy did not play *quietos* in the dirt with the other children. *Quietos* is a game of freeze where you turn your enemies to stone. A game that the young *hermanos* of Mexico grow up to play for real. Instead, The Boy left the *barrio* with a stale *tortilla* folded in his pocket. He walked down the mountain and into the city. When he arrived at the plaza he set up his shoe-shining kit and waited. Before long, an Old German appeared.

How much for a shine?

Fifteen pesos, Señor.

The Old German scowled and turned away.

Today a special price for you, Señor! Only ten pesos!

Still scowling, The Old German put his foot on the box and The Boy set to work. When The Boy had finished he said…

Are you hungry, boy?

I am always hungry, Señor.

Come with me.

And so The Boy packed up his shoe-shining kit and followed The Old German through the streets. As it grew dark they came to his butcher's shop. Here The Boy grew nervous.

You're hungry, aren't you?

Yes, Señor!

Come inside and I'll feed you.

So The Boy, listening to his growling belly, followed The Old German inside. As he stepped over the threshold of the shop he saw two *resistoleros,* the ones who sniff glue to forget, even their own names. The Boy turned to run but the *resistoleros* blocked his way. Before he could cry out, The Old German sliced The Boy's stomach wide open with a carving knife. The Boy watched with great surprise as his blood and viscera flooded the floor of the shop.

As the *resistoleros* stared glassy-eyed and wiped their noses on their shirts, The Old German deftly gutted The Boy like a *pollito*.

When The Boy's belly was entirely empty of intestines, The Old German began to pack the cavity with small white packages.

Perhaps you can guess what was in them?

The Old German then stitched the wound shut and dressed him in new clothes. He put new shoes on The Boy's little feet and a new hat on his little head. When he was finished The Boy was dressed better than he had ever been in his life. Looking at him you would think that he was only sleeping peacefully and not dead at all.

The Old German's cunning plan was to send the *resistoleros* across the border with their brother asleep in the back of the car. When they had safely crossed into the United States of America, they would cut open the stitches, remove the precious contents and dump his little body in the desert where coyotes would gnaw on his bones until they were dust.

Now as Mexican luck would have it, the *resistoleros* were stopped at the border. The guard ordered the boys from the car. Of course one of them would not, could not wake up.

On the wings of many miracles, The Boy's body was returned to his *barrio* home. The Mother wept and wept and wept and before long her tears of grief and rage filled a large cooking pot. In this cooking pot of tears The Mother made *mole negro*, a rich Oaxacan sauce from a recipe passed down from *madre* to *madre* to *madre* since before the Spanish came with their raping cocks.

To the pot, The Mother added cinnamon, garlic, banana, onion, fat, raisins, thyme and the most powerful ingredient of all, Coca-Cola.

When the *mole* was rich and ready, The Mother filled her dead son's belly with the black sauce. The other women in the *barrio* clucked their tongues. After all there were living children who were starving and in need of sustenance. But The Mother, in her grief, in her rage, paid no heed to her neighbours.

The Mother took her best needle and thread and stitched up the belly of her child with fine stitches. Each time she pierced her son's cold flesh she winced as if he could still feel the needle's prick.

When she was done The Boy appeared almost alive.

Now The Mother knelt on the dirt floor and prayed, not to Our Lady of Guadalupe, no, she prayed to Santa Muerte, Our Lady of Death.

That evening the guests arrived for the *velorio*. There were to be nine nights of storytelling and drinking. After this time the dead could finally be laid to rest.

On the first night when all the guests were asleep, the dead boy sat up and asked for a Coca-Cola. The guests fled the house in terror but The Mother embraced her blessed son and wept tears of joy. Santa Muerte had answered her prayers. The Mother swore from this day forth she would worship Santa Muerte and no other.

Now The Boy lived but he was no longer a sweet *angelito*. Instead he was filled with a rage like a young cock in the *pellea de gallos*. The Boy became known as *El Gallito*, The Little Rooster. *El Gallito* grew up to be the most fearsome cartel leader in all of Mexico. While the people feared *El Gallito*, they also loved him, especially when he ordered his hired *sicarios* to throw truckloads of pesos into the streets for the poor to peck like hungry hens. *El Gallito* was rich and powerful and had come from nothing, from dirt just like them. If The Little Rooster could make it, why couldn't they?

And no-one, not even Santa Muerte, could bleed *La Madre*'s hatred of The Old German, he who had slaughtered her son like a *pollito* in that butcher's shop, so long ago in Mexico.

And so began a war that would have no end.

And we are in:

MONTE AND SCARLET'S HOME, WOOLLAHRA

An affluent residence.

A purple piñata pony stands on a table.

JIMMY *enters, drinking a can of Coca-Cola.*

OLIVER *enters, wearing a blindfold and swinging a piñata stick, bashing everything in his way.*

As OLIVER *whacks,* JIMMY *screams in mock pain.*

OLIVER *whacks again.*

JIMMY *screams.*

OLIVER *goes to whack again but* JIMMY *grabs the stick.*

JIMMY: Hey.

OLIVER *lifts his blindfold and swings around to discover* JIMMY.

OLIVER: I'm having a P party.
JIMMY: I know.
OLIVER: You had to dress up as something beginning with P.
JIMMY: I did.
OLIVER: What?
JIMMY: Guess.
OLIVER: —
JIMMY: Come on, starts with P—
OLIVER: —
JIMMY: —ends in 'ooper'…
OLIVER: —

ACT ONE

JIMMY: Give up?
   I'm a Party Pooper.
OLIVER: That's a bit pathetic.
JIMMY: So what are you?
OLIVER: I'm a Prince.
JIMMY: Perfect.
OLIVER: Is that my present?
JIMMY: Uh-uh. This is for Ivan.
OLIVER: Who's Ivan?
JIMMY: Your twin brother.
   The good one.
OLIVER: I don't have a twin brother.
JIMMY: What have you done with Ivan?
OLIVER: Nothing.
JIMMY: You've chopped him up and fed him to the goldfish.
OLIVER: Have not.
JIMMY: Have so, psycho.
OLIVER: I haven't.
JIMMY: Well I guess if Ivan's cactus you might as well have his present.
OLIVER: What is it?
JIMMY: Open it.

> OLIVER *rips into the paper and reveals a toy pistol. He aims it at* JIMMY.

OLIVER: Freeze!
JIMMY: Don't shoot, I'm too young to die.

> OLIVER *pumps several rounds into* JIMMY.
>
> JIMMY *dies.*
>
> OLIVER *takes the opportunity to take a sip from* JIMMY*'s Coke while prodding* JIMMY*'s body with his foot.*
>
> JIMMY *is still.*
>
> OLIVER *prods him again.* JIMMY *wakes from the dead and grabs* OLIVER.

   Like?
OLIVER: Best present ever.

JIMMY: Okay, run along and massacre your friends then.

> OLIVER *runs off firing shots.*
>
> JIMMY *mimes wringing* OLIVER*'s neck.*
>
> JIMMY *finishes his Coke and crushes the can.*
>
> SCARLET, *four months pregnant, enters with the toy pistol behind her back.*
>
> *She holds the gun to* JIMMY*'s head.*

SCARLET: Freeze mother-fucker.

> JIMMY *freezes.*

What's this?

JIMMY: Never seen it before in my life.

SCARLET: The truth, Jimmy, or you get it.

JIMMY: It's a toy—

SCARLET: Jimmy…

JIMMY: —it's just pretend.

SCARLET: What voice in your head said a replica pistol is an appropriate gift for a seven-year-old boy?

JIMMY: I would have killed for one of those when I was a kid.

SCARLET: He's not keeping it.

JIMMY: Seriously?

SCARLET: He has an overactive imagination.

JIMMY: Gets that from me.

SCARLET: Unfortunately.

JIMMY: I fucked up?

SCARLET: I wish you'd run it by me, Jimmy.

JIMMY: Sorry.

SCARLET: I'd like to believe he's been given so many presents today that he'll forget this one.

JIMMY: No?

SCARLET: Not a chance.

JIMMY: I'm really fucking sorry.

SCARLET: Why are you so cute?

> SCARLET *kisses* JIMMY *on the lips.*

JIMMY: Sorry.

ACT ONE

SCARLET: Just like Oliver, you get away with murder.
JIMMY: Next birthday I'll get him something really boring.
   I'll get him a book. About tax.
SCARLET: Perfect.
   Now can you please get rid of it?

     JIMMY *puts the gun in his jeans.*

JIMMY: Need a hand?
SCARLET: Caterers.
JIMMY: Can I just say, sister of mine, you are living the dream.
SCARLET: You get used to it.
JIMMY: I could get used to it.
SCARLET: Hey, got—
JIMMY: No.
   No.
SCARLET: Your eyelashes flutter when you lie.
JIMMY: Seriously I'm out.
SCARLET: Do I have to tickle you to death?

     JIMMY *hands over a cigarette.*

   Keep an eye out.

     JIMMY *checks for* MONTE.

JIMMY: Close your eyes.
SCARLET: Why?
JIMMY: Close your eyes, hold out your hand.
SCARLET: Jimmy, is this some trick?
JIMMY: No trick.

     JIMMY *places an expensive piece of jewellery in* SCARLET*'s hand.*

   Open.
SCARLET: What's this?
JIMMY: It's a gift.
SCARLET: It's not my birthday.
JIMMY: So?
SCARLET: Jimmy—
JIMMY: You like it?
SCARLET: I can't take this.

JIMMY: You hate it—
SCARLET: No.
JIMMY: —I can take it / back.
SCARLET: No it's lovely but you / can't.
JIMMY: Can.
SCARLET: How?
JIMMY: Let's just say it was massively marked down, do you like it?
SCARLET: —
JIMMY: It's to thank you.
SCARLET: For?
JIMMY: All the shit you've done / for me.
SCARLET: You don't have to do this, Jimmy.
JIMMY: I want to.
SCARLET: I can't, Jimmy, / no I'm sorry.
JIMMY: Take it. Please. Please?

    Pause.

SCARLET: Thanks. [*Pause.*] How's TAFE?
JIMMY: TAFE is terrific.
SCARLET: You're getting something out of it?
JIMMY: Last week I learnt how to work an Excel spreadsheet.
SCARLET: That's a life skill.
JIMMY: This week M.Y.O.B. cannot fucking wait.
SCARLET: You want Monte to trust you, don't you?
JIMMY: Yeah.
SCARLET: So graduate and he might let you run the deli in Ultimo.
JIMMY: Yeah. Great.

    Pause.

SCARLET: You're well?
JIMMY: I am.
SCARLET: You sure?
JIMMY: Positive.

    Pause.

SCARLET: Just checking in.
JIMMY: I know.
SCARLET: I have to / ask.

JIMMY: Yuh.
SCARLET: You'd tell me?
JIMMY: Scout's honour.

   Pause.

SCARLET: Can't have you in / this house if you're—
JIMMY: I'm not.
SCARLET: You understand / why.
JIMMY: I know the rules
SCARLET: / Jimmy?
JIMMY: I fucking love this family.
SCARLET: Good.
  Because we don't want to lose you again.

    MONTE *enters, driving a remote-control BMW.* SCARLET *passes the lit cigarette to* JIMMY.

  What have I said about smoking in the house, Jimmy—

    JIMMY *looks for a place to extinguish the cigarette.*

JIMMY: Sorry.
SCARLET: —especially with the baby—
JIMMY: Shit shit, sorry.
SCARLET: —and new research suggests even second-hand smoke may harm the foetus.
JIMMY: I did not know that.
SCARLET: Well, you do now.
JIMMY: Thanks.
  Monte.
  Sorry.

    MONTE *stares at* JIMMY.

MONTE: Don't smoke in the house, / bro.
JIMMY: No.
MONTE: You know the rules.
JIMMY: Won't happen again, what's this?
MONTE: Replica BMW M6 convertible.
JIMMY: Beauty.
MONTE: Oliver's present. Custom built by yours truly.

JIMMY: Give one of those to me if you like, Monte.
MONTE: Can I just?
JIMMY: Just supersize it.
SCARLET: Oliver hasn't had a chance to play with it yet.
MONTE: It's not really a toy, baby.
SCARLET: Monte's been hogging it all morning.
MONTE: Instructing him how to operate it safely, Scarlet.
    Can't believe he's eight.
JIMMY & SCARLET: [*together*] Seven.
MONTE: Fuck. Baby, do you have the skywriter's mobile number?
SCARLET: Monte, no no you / can't be….
MONTE: It's a joke, Scarlet.
    I know how old my firstborn is, give me some credit.
SCARLET: Very funny, he's funny, isn't he, Jimmy?
MONTE: It's all sorted.
    He's flying over Woollahra in… fifteen minutes.
SCARLET: Happy seventh birthday, Oliver?
MONTE: Word for word.
JIMMY: Lucky boy.
SCARLET: God it scares me.
MONTE: What scares you, baby?
SCARLET: His childhood disappearing.
    Remember the day he was conceived?
JIMMY: / Okay I might head outside…

    JIMMY *heads out,* MONTE *grabs him.*

MONTE: I want a word with you.
SCARLET: Day of your dad's funeral.
MONTE: That's right.
SCARLET: Tell Jimmy the story.
MONTE: About how we met at the Ivy—
SCARLET: / Not that story.
JIMMY: I've heard that story.
MONTE: —and I rented the bikini?
JIMMY: / A hundred and fifty bucks.
MONTE: A hundred and fifty bucks to hire a bikini for a swim with the hottest hostess in the house. It was worth it. Every. Sexy. Cent.

ACT ONE

Pause.

SCARLET: Not that story, Monte.
MONTE: Fine.
SCARLET: So we came home from the funeral—
MONTE: —ripped our clothes off went for it.
SCARLET: You cried.
MONTE: Excuse me?
SCARLET: Your father had just died.
MONTE: Baby—
SCARLET: It was really—

MONTE grabs SCARLET and puts his hands over her mouth.

MONTE: Baby…
SCARLET: —beautiful.
MONTE: / Get the gaffa, will you, Jimmy?
SCARLET: Monte, don't don't, Jimmy help, Jimmy help me.

JIMMY does nothing.

I could lose the baby.

MONTE lets go.

Bully.
MONTE: So we screwed. It was hot. More potent than oysters.
SCARLET: What?
MONTE: Funerals. Aphrodisiacs, / death—
SCARLET: No.
MONTE: —and sex yes.
SCARLET: That's disgusting.

Pause.

MONTE: / Anyway.
SCARLET: Anyway.

SCARLET grabs JIMMY and tells the story to him.

After, we lay there—
MONTE: —post-coital—
SCARLET: —half asleep.

The afternoon sun came through the window and I watched the light passing over my body… over here…

SCARLET *takes* JIMMY*'s hand in hers and places it on her pregnant belly.*

And I knew.

I said to Monte—

MONTE: —I'm pregnant.

SCARLET: And I was.

Pause.

JIMMY: Wow.

Magic.

MONTE: What's this?

SCARLET: Oh, it's a gift.

From Jimmy.

MONTE *laughs.*

JIMMY: What?

MONTE: You wasted your money, bro. She'll never wear it.

SCARLET *a takes the piñata and heads out.*

SCARLET: Time for the *piñata*?

MONTE: We'll be out in a sec, baby.

SCARLET *stops.*

SCARLET: Everyone's waiting, Monte.

MONTE: I just want a quick word with Jimmy.

Pause.

SCARLET *looks at* JIMMY, *then leaves with the piñata.*

Cheeky Charlie?

Beat.

JIMMY: I'm on the softies thanks, Monte.

MONTE: Course you are, keep forgetting.

Happy to fly solo.

MONTE *prepares the cocaine on the bench.*

How's the Penrith pad?

JIMMY: I'm thinking of printing 'I heart Penrif' t-shirts.

Selling them for ten bucks a piece down at Penrif Plaza.

Reckon I could make a mint.

MONTE: And the Mazda?
JIMMY: Magda?
MONTE: Haven't pranged it yet?
JIMMY: Kid gloves.
MONTE: I should hope so.
JIMMY: And as much as I love the old girl I reckon a Beemer's more my style.
MONTE: Cocky little shit.
JIMMY: It's my hormones, can't help it.
MONTE: Listen, Jimmy.

>OLIVER *runs in.* MONTE *shields the coke.*

OLIVER: Daddy?
MONTE: What is it, little prince?
OLIVER: Come and watch me bash the *piñata*.
MONTE: In a minute.
OLIVER: Now.
MONTE: Bossy little prince.
> I'm the king remember.
OLIVER: No you're not.
MONTE: Yes I am.
> I'm the king, you're the prince, and you know what that means?
> One day you'll get everything.
OLIVER: What do I get?
MONTE: My entire kingdom.
OLIVER: Yes.
MONTE: Yeah, you like the sound of that?
OLIVER: What about Uncle Jimmy?
MONTE: What about him?
OLIVER: Is Uncle Jimmy a prince?
JIMMY: Yeah, am I a prince, Monte?
MONTE: He's more of a knight.
OLIVER: Does he get any of your kingdom?
MONTE: He might.

>JIMMY *pokes his tongue at* OLIVER.

> If he behaves himself.

>MONTE *slaps* JIMMY *on the arse.*

OLIVER *spots* MONTE*'s cocaine.*

OLIVER: Is that sugar?

OLIVER *reaches for it,* JIMMY *grabs his hand.*

MONTE: Nope.
OLIVER: We quit sugar.
MONTE: It's not sugar, now go outside, hey. We'll be out in a minute.
OLIVER: No.

OLIVER *grabs the toy pistol from* JIMMY*'s jeans and points it at* MONTE.

MONTE: Go.

OLIVER *runs off.*

It's like he reaches his little hand down my throat and rips out my still-beating heart.
JIMMY: Sounds painful.
MONTE: It is, bro. Fathering is emotional fucking torture.

MONTE *snorts another cap of coke.*

You want this?
JIMMY: [*thinking he means the coke*] I already said, / Monte, I'm not…
MONTE: No, Jimmy, all this.

Everything I have.

Beemer…

House on the harbour…

Private fucking beach…
JIMMY: You don't have a house on the harbour, Monte…
MONTE: —
JIMMY: … or a private fucking beach… [*Beat.*] Do you?
MONTE: I'm asking you, do you / want it?
JIMMY: I want it.

I fucking want it.
MONTE: How would you like to come with me to Berlin?
JIMMY: Get fucked, how come?
MONTE: Quinoa.
JIMMY: Quinoa?
MONTE: I've got a meeting with an organic wholesaler in Kruezberg.

ACT ONE

Pause.

JIMMY: Yeah right.
MONTE: There's been a game change, Jimmy.
JIMMY: Since when?
MONTE: Since the rumour La Madre has cancer.
JIMMY: La Madre has cancer?
MONTE: Wanna tell Woollahra?
JIMMY: You fucking serious?
MONTE: Word on the street she's got three months.
So I'm keen to set up a new deal before she kicks it.
JIMMY: Direct?
MONTE: You in?
JIMMY: Scarlet…?
MONTE: What are you studying at TAFE again?
JIMMY: Business communications.
MONTE: School excursion.
JIMMY: Yeah, but won't she—?
MONTE: No.
You might learn something. Are you in, Jimmy?
JIMMY: Will there be leisure time 'cause I've heard about this club called Berghain, / it's really hard to get in.
MONTE: Yeah, we'll see what we can schedule. Are you in, Jimmy?
JIMMY: Fuck. Yes.
MONTE: Piñata?

MONTE leaves.

JIMMY: Piñata!

The sound of an aeroplane overhead.

JIMMY is suddenly, violently ill.

He doubles over with stomach cramps.

The world spins.

A purple piñata looms above him.

OLIVER swings at the piñata with the stick.

His hits become increasingly violent.

The piñata splits.

Time shift.

JIMMY wakes. He looks terrible.

OLIVER hovers over JIMMY.

JIMMY notices OLIVER's shoes.

Where'd you get those?

OLIVER looks down at his shoes.

SCARLET enters.

SCARLET: Leave Uncle Jimmy alone, he's not well.

OLIVER runs out.

SCARLET feels JIMMY's forehead.

How you feeling?

JIMMY nods.

Monte's going to drive you home, okay.

Poor Jimmy, first overseas trip and he comes back sick.

Pause.

How was Berlin? You learn something?

JIMMY goes to speak as MONTE enters.

MONTE: I learnt something.

The delicate art of foreign diplomacy when your travelling companion projectile vomits over the New Zealand rugby team during a long-haul flight.

SCARLET: Not much fun.

MONTE: The highlight of the trip for me was when Jimmy shat his shoes in customs.

SCARLET: No.

MONTE: That put a shine on everyone's face.

Nice one, bro.

SCARLET: Poor Jimmy.

JIMMY: Thanks for sharing, Monte.

MONTE: Ready to roll?

SCARLET: You'll call if you get any worse?

Promise?

ACT ONE 17

JIMMY *nods.*

SCARLET *exits.*

MONTE: Didn't mention Bolivia, did you?

JIMMY *shakes his head.*

Don't. Let's go. We'll drop in on Christos on the way over.
JIMMY: Monte.
MONTE: ?

JIMMY *is silent.*

What?
JIMMY: What if we don't do this?
MONTE: Done it.
JIMMY: You could change your mind.
MONTE: Thank you for your permission, Jimmy.
JIMMY: I feel sick.
Feel sick about it.
MONTE: That's the Aztec's Curse. Montezuma's Revenge. Pop a few Imodium and it'll clear right up.
JIMMY: It's sick over there, Monte, it's fucked up—
MONTE: Hey, I didn't love having to go there.
JIMMY: —that kid—
MONTE: You didn't say anything to Scarlet?
JIMMY: ?
MONTE: The kid. In Bolivia?
JIMMY: No.
I can't stop.
MONTE: Hey. Keep your eyes on the road ahead. Don't look back. Keep your mind on the prize. Yeah?
JIMMY: Yeah.
MONTE: Do not mention this again. Clear?
JIMMY: Yeah but—
MONTE: I am trying to help you, Jimmy. I am trying to give you a leg-up, can you see that?
JIMMY: Yeah.
MONTE: The TAFE course, / yeah?
JIMMY: Yeah, I know / I know.

MONTE: The one-bedder, the car, / the works…
JIMMY: I appreciate all that.
MONTE: I don't think you do, Jimmy.
JIMMY: I do, Monte, / I really—
MONTE: In this city if you don't get a leg-up you drown.
JIMMY: Yeah, I know / I know.
MONTE: So quit dogpaddling. You want to buy a place round here, yeah?
JIMMY: Yeah.
MONTE: There's a magic eight kay radius. Sydney is shit if you live outside of it. You don't want to be back and forth across the city every time you want to see the family, see Oli.
JIMMY: / No.
MONTE: So what are you doing about it? What's your plan?
JIMMY: I've been saving.
MONTE: Have you mate that's great.

    I'll bet my son has more in his piggy bank.

JIMMY: I've got / a bit more than…
MONTE: You know what your problem is?

    Look in the mirror.

    You dress like some white trash hood.

    Still stuck in your sad old junkie story.

    Ends badly that story, Jimmy, ends very badly for you.

    This version's different.

    You grow up.

    Let's go.

    And don't shit in the Merc.

> JIMMY *doubles up with a wave of stomach cramp.*

JIMMY: No, Monte.

> *And we are in:*

THE NORTHCOTT HOUSING ESTATE, SURRY HILLS

CHRISTOS LYMBIOUS *answers the door to* MONTE *and* JIMMY.

MONTE: Christos Jimmy, Jimmy Christos.

    Jimmy needs the bathroom.

ACT ONE

CHRISTOS: No, fuck off.
MONTE: Come on, Christos.
CHRISTOS: Use the one in the park.
MONTE: Don't think he'll make it that far.
CHRISTOS: Made it up ten flights, didn't he?
JIMMY: I won't make it.
MONTE: Show some mercy.
    Pause.
CHRISTOS: Be quick about it.
    JIMMY *darts past* CHRISTOS *and exits to the toilet.*
Who's the kid?
MONTE: Jimmy.
CHRISTOS: Skinny?
MONTE: Jimmy.
CHRISTOS: Who's feeding him?
MONTE: I am.
CHRISTOS: I see.
MONTE: He's family.
CHRISTOS: Is he?
MONTE: Where's Petra?
CHRISTOS: Having a lie down.
MONTE: So you're living here now?
CHRISTOS: It's temporary.
MONTE: You're not sleeping in there are you?
CHRISTOS: Hey?
MONTE: You're not sleeping in the bed with your old mum? / I know what you Greek boys are like.
CHRISTOS: Fuck off, Monte, fuck off.
MONTE: No it's nice.
  It's really nice.
  Love the public housing look.
    CHRISTOS *exits to the balcony.*
  Where you going? You're not going to jump, are you? You're not that sorry to see me?
CHRISTOS: Where's your car, where'd you park it?

MONTE: In the carpark, where do you think? You try finding a park in Surry Hills.
CHRISTOS: In my space?
MONTE: Where's your space?
CHRISTOS: You did, you prick, you parked your brand new fucking Merc in my fucking car space.
MONTE: What's the problem?

    CHRISTOS *calls out.*

CHRISTOS: Skinny, finish up!
MONTE: Jimmy.

    JIMMY *calls out.*

JIMMY: [*offstage*] What?!
CHRISTOS: Tie a knot, Skinny, Monte's off.
MONTE: What's the problem?
CHRISTOS: I don't need the fucking attention.
MONTE: Come on, Christos, turn the paranoia down a notch.
CHRISTOS: You don't fucking live here.
MONTE: If I did I'd be first over the balcony.
CHRISTOS: Gossip runs through these towers like / you wouldn't…
MONTE: Diarrhea?
CHRISTOS: Yeah yeah, just like diarrhoea.

    Someone sees a brand new Merc in my car space suddenly I'm back on the game.

MONTE: What if you were?

    Beat.

CHRISTOS: You have to be fucking—

    MONTE *reveals a bag of coke and starts to cut it with his credit card.*

    No no, not here, not fucking here.

MONTE: Honestly? I preferred your old place on the harbour.
CHRISTOS: How long is he gunna be?
MONTE: Bali belly, you know the story. What's on the box?

    MONTE *grabs the remote and turns the volume up on the TV. It's* 'Who Wants to be a Millionaire'.

ACT ONE 21

This should be 'Who Wants to be a Billionaire'.
What can you buy for a million dollars these days?
Terrace in Tempe with rising damp.

> MONTE *snorts a line.*

CHRISTOS: Jesus, Monte, my bloody mum's in there.
MONTE: You still in touch with the boys in baggage?
CHRISTOS: Here we go.

> MONTE *sings.*

MONTE: [*singing*] I've been to cities that never shut down,
From New York to Rome to old London town
But no matter how far or how wide I roam,
I still call Australia…
Sing it with me, Christos.
[*Singing*] Yes, I still call Australia…
CHRISTOS: You finished?
MONTE: [*singing*] … home.
CHRISTOS: I think you'll find they've updated their song.
MONTE: Is that correct?
CHRISTOS: That's the Qantas theme song of the Sydney 2000 Olympics.
MONTE: You see this is exactly why I come to you, Christos. I come to you because you are the leading authority on the inner workings of Qantas Limited.
CHRISTOS: No.
MONTE: No to what?
CHRISTOS: No to what you're about to ask me.
MONTE: Why don't you have a line—
CHRISTOS: You got shit in your ears?
MONTE: —unwind?
CHRISTOS: I'm off the parrot.
MONTE: No you're not, the parrot is sitting right there on your shoulder, squawking its head off giving me an earache.
So…

> MONTE *offers the line to* CHRISTOS.

… give Polly a cracker and we can hear ourselves talk.

> CHRISTOS *eyes the line.*

CHRISTOS: I've got Mum to think of now.
MONTE: Of course you do.
CHRISTOS: You know she had a stroke while I was inside?
MONTE: Sorry to hear that.
CHRISTOS: If I hadn't got early parole she'd still be in the nursing home. Worse than the nick some of those shit holes.
MONTE: You're a good Greek son.
CHRISTOS: Taken me months to get her talking again.
She still can't move her left side.
We're working on that, every day, bit by bit.
Meanwhile I'm taking her to the toilet, bathing her, heating up her Meals on Wheels.
MONTE: That's what I can smell. Thought it was dog food.
CHRISTOS: You prick.
MONTE: Have you got one of those chairs?
CHRISTOS: Have I got what?
MONTE: You know those remote-control chairs for your mum?
CHRISTOS: No.
MONTE: I'll order one.
CHRISTOS: Don't.
MONTE: I'm ordering one.

> MONTE *pulls out his mobile phone.*

CHRISTOS: Don't fucking want it.
MONTE: I'll have it delivered tomorrow.
CHRISTOS: She's alright. I help her up and down.
MONTE: What about when you're not here, what about when you're stoned down the Shakespeare?
CHRISTOS: Not my scene, Monte.
MONTE: Since when?
CHRISTOS: Since God granted me the serenity to accept the things I cannot fucking change.
MONTE: What language are you speaking?
CHRISTOS: Not a language you'd understand.
MONTE: —
CHRISTOS: N.A. seven days a week.

> JIMMY *appears, pulling up his jeans.*

ACT ONE

Okay, thank you both for the surprise / visit.
JIMMY: Oh wait, wait.

    JIMMY *races back to the toilet.*

CHRISTOS: Use the freshener, Skinny!
MONTE: How's business?
CHRISTOS: You fucking know.
MONTE: I believed in you.
CHRISTOS: That was good of you, Monte.
MONTE: Why would I front two hundred grand for a B-grade idea?
CHRISTOS: You would if it was in your interest.
MONTE: You had a dream.
CHRISTOS: The world shits on dreams.
MONTE: So you build dreams out of shit.
CHRISTOS: Yeah, you're good at that.

    You're the architect of crap.
MONTE: You were on a winner.
CHRISTOS: Winner was it? Your fucking laundromat?
MONTE: It was the go-to bar in Randwick.

    The post-race place for champagne and cocaine.
CHRISTOS: A.C.C. made a tidy profit from it.
MONTE: We both lost.
CHRISTOS: I lost a fuckload more than you / so don't…
MONTE: / True true.

    And I owe you.

    I know that.
CHRISTOS: Fuck off and we'll call it quits.

    Pause.

MONTE: How far up are we?
CHRISTOS: There's the door.
MONTE: How many floors? Nine, ten?
CHRISTOS: Ten.
MONTE: You can see the bridge from here can't you?
CHRISTOS: Wrong side.
MONTE: That's a pity.

    Other day I'm driving over the bridge and I hear this story on the radio.

Athens. Fifty-five-year-old man jumps out of a fifteen-story apartment block—
CHRISTOS: So fuckin' what?
MONTE: —with his ninety-year-old mum in his arms.
She had dementia. He was taking care of her after he'd lost his job. Up… and over.
Now that is a Greek tragedy. And you're another. You don't belong here, Christos. You deserve that view of the harbour. You and your mother.
CHRISTOS: I get put away again, what happens to her?
MONTE: I've got a green light.

JIMMY *returns to the room.*

CHRISTOS: You cocky little blue-blood prick.
Seven years.
Seven fucking years inside.
Everything I had, taken, proceeds of crime.
A.C.C. didn't give a flying fuck if it was or wasn't, seized the fucking lot plus some of my mum's stuff.
I could have got off with a lot less time, a lot fucking less with a roll and you fucking know it.
You're lucky I'm not a dog.
So don't you come here acting like you're my fairy fucking godmother.
I'll knock your fucking head off.

MONTE *and* CHRISTOS *see* JIMMY.

You use the freshener?
JIMMY: Me?
CHRISTOS: Who do you think I'm talking to?
JIMMY: I'd leave it a bit.

MONTE *tosses a key at* CHRISTOS.

CHRISTOS: What's this?
MONTE: Key.
CHRISTOS: To your heart is it Monte?
MONTE: Better.
CHRISTOS: Can't imagine.
MONTE: Apartment in Darlinghurst.

ACT ONE 25

JIMMY: I didn't know you had a place in Darlinghurst, Monte.
MONTE: Stunning views. Top floor. Three bed. Two bath. Polished floors. European appliances.
CHRISTOS: What more could you want?
JIMMY: Better than my shit box in Penrith.
CHRISTOS: Why you giving this key to me, Monte?
MONTE: Move your mum in Monday.

Beat.

CHRISTOS: How long?
MONTE: Indefinitely.
To be honest I feel guilty.
CHRISTOS: There's hope in the world yet.
MONTE: Homeless crisis in the city and I've got a place in the C.B.D. sitting empty.
JIMMY: I'll take it if you don't want it, Christos.
MONTE & CHRISTOS: [*together*] Shut up.
CHRISTOS: Cough up the catch.
MONTE: I respect the fact that you've retired.
CHRISTOS: Do you now?
MONTE: I think you deserve your gold watch. [*Pause.*] You do the first two pick-ups then a lump sum to deal direct with your contact at Qantas. Jimmy here takes the reigns and you live happily ever after.
CHRISTOS: You in this too, Skinny?

JIMMY *nods.*

Watch your back.
MONTE: Jimmy's family.
JIMMY: I'm family.

Pause.

CHRISTOS: How's it coming in?
MONTE: Lan Chile flight from Santiago.
CHRISTOS: Unaccompanied?
MONTE: Courier.
CHRISTOS: Who's the desperado?
MONTE: Their end.
CHRISTOS: Santiago direct?
MONTE: Correct.

CHRISTOS: Not La Madre then?
MONTE: No.
CHRISTOS: Not La Madre's amigos?
MONTE: What did I just say?

Beat.

CHRISTOS: This kosher?
MONTE: What do you know from kosher, Christos?
CHRISTOS: Does La Madre fucking know?
MONTE: Don't worry about La Madre.
CHRISTOS: You got a death wish?
MONTE: La Madre's got other things on her mind.
CHRISTOS: Like?
MONTE: Stage-four stomach cancer.
CHRISTOS: Momento fucking mori.

CHRISTOS *crosses himself.*

MONTE: You see our opportunity?

Pause.

CHRISTOS: When's the pick-up?
MONTE: Next month.

CHRISTOS *is silent.*

Anyway have a think.

And I am leaving you this one anorexic line for old times.

And we are in:

OLIVER'S BEDROOM, WOOLLAHRA

OLIVER *wakes suddenly from a nightmare.*
In darkness he goes to a wall and begins to draw.
Simultaneously we are in:

THE LIVERPOOL MEGACENTRE FOOD COURT

JIMMY *sits at a table, texting. A dozen-box of Krispy Kreme donuts are in front of him.*

JIMMY *is plagued with chronic stomach cramps.*

ACT ONE

DETECTIVE GRUBBE *takes a seat at* JIMMY*'s table.*

GRUBBE: There aren't too many places you can buy two dozen Krispy Kreme original glazed these days.

Here at the Liverpool Megacentre you can.

Qantas departure / lounge—

JIMMY: Fuck off, I'm busy.

GRUBBE: I noticed. I've been watching this spot run hot for the last hour. Why pay the overheads on office space when the largest homeware centre in the Southern Hemisphere is the perfect cover?

I'm sorry, have I interrupted your morning tea, Jimmy?

Go on, have a donut, don't mind me.

Pause.

JIMMY: Not hungry.

GRUBBE: You're as pale as a sheet, Jimmy, you've lost all your colour.

JIMMY: Who are you?

GRUBBE: It's a common mythology that cops love donuts.

Like a mouse loves cheese, like a rabbit loves a carrot.

But that's an American motif I find quite offensive.

Personally I wouldn't touch one of those if you held a gun to my head.

Full of fat and sugar, the silent killers.

JIMMY: Listen—

GRUBBE: You're listening to me, Jimmy.

You might remember that at one time, back in the mid naughties, people would travel miles to sink their teeth into a Krispy Kreme original glazed.

Indeed it was not uncommon to see people returning on aeroplanes to Brisbane and Melbourne with a mixed dozen in a box just like this one. When customers travel to you as a retailer of non-essential items it's easy to believe that broad expansion is not only possible, it's inevitable. Tragically the expansion of Krispy Kreme was far too wide, far too rapid. The company was destined for disaster. Krispy Kreme Incorporated had a death wish.

You can use that economic thesis for one of your TAFE assignments. You could call it 'The Hole in Krispy Kreme's Business Plan'.

How's the TAFE course going, Jimmy?

JIMMY *doubles up with stomach pain.*

Took time off recently?

Yeah, Jimmy, I know about your trip.

You see I get a little pop-up on my computer when persons of interest enter or exit the country, especially from hot spots like South America. The pop-up makes a little noise.

A bit like a… well it's a bit like a…

GRUBBE *makes the sound.*

Makes my day. Business or pleasure?

JIMMY: I don't have to say shit.

GRUBBE: That's true.

JIMMY: I could walk.

GRUBBE: Go on give it a go.

JIMMY *doesn't move.*

Did you pick up a bug in Bolivia, Jimmy?

Is that why you're off-colour?

Was it the guinea pig?

Could have been the *mate*, water doesn't boil at a hundred degrees in high altitudes.

That bug'll stay in your stomach until you purge it.

It'll rear up and strike when the climate's just right.

Gastro's a lot like fascism.

You watch TV, Jimmy?

JIMMY: What?

GRUBBE: You probably watch a lot of crime shows?

Have you noticed how the bad guys have something in common?

JIMMY: Yeah, what?

GRUBBE: *Mortido*. Do you know what that is, Jimmy?

JIMMY: Nuh.

GRUBBE: I have it.

You have it.

The shareholders of Krispy Kreme Inc. have it.

The death instinct. The desire for self-destruction.

Not my idea.

Sigmund Freud's. Heard of him?

JIMMY: Yeah, I've heard of the cunt.
GRUBBE: You've heard of the cunt, very good.
Freud reckoned love and hate, sex and death are twin impulses.
The act of consumption gives life to the consumer but destroys the consumed.
Kind of what happens when you eat a donut.
You live, but you destroy the original glazed.
Existence is an endless circle of life and death, life and death.
But ultimately, the aim of all life is self-destruction.
That's *mortido*, Jimmy.
JIMMY: Are you fucking serious?
GRUBBE: Well that depends on what's in the box. [*Pause.*] Your record, I could put you away for eight to ten.
JIMMY: So what's with the foreplay? Why don't you just fuck me?
GRUBBE: Oh well, it's more fun this way.
JIMMY: Where's the backup?

> JIMMY *looks around the food court.*

GRUBBE: How do you know those pensioners enjoying a muffin break over there aren't undercover cops?
JIMMY: Yeah? So fuckin' nail me.
GRUBBE: I'd love to but you're nothing but a meat puppet in the scheme of things.
You don't pull the strings, do you, Jimmy?
JIMMY: —
GRUBBE: No. So in situations like this Mr Bing Lee knows best.
JIMMY: Who the fuck's Bing Lee?
GRUBBE: Bing Lee furniture store.
Level four.
Where Everything's Negotiable!
What do you think, Jimmy?
Are you ready to negotiate?

> GRUBBE *pushes his card across the table.* JIMMY *stares at it for a moment, then quickly shoves it in his pocket.*

IN OLIVER'S BEDROOM

SCARLET *enters to discover* OLIVER *has drawn a picture of a rooster in lipstick on one of the walls.*

SCARLET: Oli?
Are you sick?
SCARLET *feels* OLIVER*'s forehead. He's burning up.*
Baby, you're burning up.
SCARLET *sees the picture of a rooster that* OLIVER *has drawn.*

END OF ACT ONE

ACT TWO

And we are in:

AN ORGANIC CAFÉ, KRUEZBERG, BERLIN

SIBYLLE, *a hipster, is working on an Apple laptop. There is a plate of cake on the table.*

MONTE: Sibylle?
SIBYLLE: *Und Du bist wer?* [You are?]
MONTE: Monte.
SIBYLLE: *Wer ist das?* [Who is this?]
MONTE: *Das is Jimmy.* [This is Jimmy.]
JIMMY: *Guten Morgan.* [Good morning.]
SIBYLLE: *Setz Dich.* [Sit.]

    They sit.

Du hast nicht gesagt dass Du einen Freund hast. [You didn't tell me you had a friend.]
MONTE: *Er kann warten draussen, wenn Dir lieber...* [He can wait outside if you'd prefer...]
SIBYLLE: *In Berlin lassen wir noch nicht mal die Hunde draussen warten.* [In Berlin we don't even make our dogs wait outside.] [*Pause.*] *Mag Dein Freund Kuchen?* [Does your friend like cake?]

    MONTE *doesn't understand.*

MONTE: Ah...
SIBYLLE: Where did you learn German?
MONTE: Clubbing in the early nineties.
SIBYLLE: This explains why your German is so *scheisse*. Why don't we speak in English?
MONTE: I'm happy to practise.
SIBYLLE: *Ja*, not on me, Monte. Jimmy, do you like cake?
JIMMY: I fucking love cake.
SIBYLLE: Are you vegan?

JIMMY: Nope.
SIBYLLE: Open.

> SIBYLLE *spoons cake into* JIMMY*'s mouth.*

Beetroot sour cream quinoa crumble. What do you think?
JIMMY: *Guten*. Very. *Guten*.
SIBYLLE: *Ja*? This is my recipe. I'm selling it in all my organic supermarkets.

> SIBYLLE *spoons more cake into* JIMMY*'s mouth.*

And what about you, Monte, how do like the quinoa?
MONTE: I love the quinoa.
JIMMY: I love the quinoa in this cake.
MONTE: There's a seriously insatiable appetite for the quinoa in Sydney.
SIBYLLE: So I hear.

Do you know in Europe right now, in Greece in Spain, it's a fucking hell hole, *ja*? There is no work so no cash for the quinoa. Everyone is too busy eating horsemeat souvlaki, shooting themselves in the head, lighting themselves on fire, beating up refugees.

And so again the fucking fascists are marching in the streets. Everything is fucking repeat.

In Australia of course you're all sucking oysters and riding fucking dolphins at Bondi Beach.

JIMMY: We don't all ride dolphins. It's an extreme sport.
SIBYLLE: You're cute.
JIMMY: Hey, have you been to a club called Berghain?
SIBYLLE: *Ja*, of course.
JIMMY: Think we'll get in?
SIBYLLE: You will, him not so much.
MONTE: Back to business?
SIBYLLE: So you know this fucking boring fucking financial crisis is why my uncle is looking for a Sydney distributer.

This is boutique Bolivian product.

High end. Packaged for the Australian market.

My uncle will only partner with the right people.
MONTE: Of course. We're a perfect fit.
SIBYLLE: Convince me.

ACT TWO

JIMMY: This cake is fucking great.

    SIBYLLE *receives an email. She reads it.*

SIBYLLE: Go.

MONTE: Okay.

Last month a Russian developer flew me to the Gold Coast in his private jet to attend a party in his penthouse apartment.

SIBYLLE: Russian developer, *ja*...

MONTE: Three days ago I had breakfast with the chairman of a major mining company and that evening dinner with a federal minister.

Before my flight I grabbed a quick latte in the Qantas lounge with a member of the Hollywood A list... who shall remain nameless.

    SIBYLLE *is emailing on her phone.*

You know what, Sibylle? You're wasting my time.

Do your research.

My clients know my name is one they can trust.

Your uncle should be gagging to do business with me.

    SIBYLLE's *email flies away. She puts down the phone.*

SIBYLLE: Okay.

MONTE: —

SIBYLLE: Now you go to Coroico.

MONTE: We go where?

SIBYLLE: In Coroico you meet my uncle.

I can email him to tell him you seem okay but my uncle has the final say.

MONTE: In Coroico?

JIMMY: Where's that?

SIBYLLE: La Paz. [*Beat.*] Bolivia? [*Beat.*] South America?

MONTE: How do we get there?

SIBYLLE: Tegel to LAX—LAX to La Paz.

MONTE: Then what?

SIBYLLE: From La Paz you take a bus or a mountain bike, whatever you like, and you go all the way down El Camino de la Muerte.

JIMMY: El Camino de la Muerte?

MONTE: What is that?

SIBYLLE: Translation?

MONTE: Yes please.
SIBYLLE: The Road of Death.
JIMMY: The road of what?
MONTE: This is a joke right? This is a German joke.
SIBYLLE: At the end of the road is the village of Coroico.
 The gateway to the Amazon… or something like this.
 You can't miss it.
MONTE: How far exactly?
SIBYLLE: Listen, Monte, I'm not going to hold your fucking hand.
 Try downloading the Google map app, Lonely fucking Planet.
MONTE: Fuck this. Jimmy?
JIMMY: What?
MONTE: We're off.
SIBYLLE: You said you wanted to deal direct?
MONTE: —
SIBYLLE: So this is where they grow the quinoa.

> SIBYLLE *kisses* JIMMY *on the lips and slips a packet of coke in his pocket.*

 Why don't you try some, *ja*?
 If you don't like it don't go.
 Okay now I play Tischtennis in Gorlitzer Park.

> SIBYLLE *picks up her table tennis racket and goes to leave.*

JIMMY: What's he like? Your uncle?
SIBYLLE: I've never met him.

> *A wave of Berlin club music.*
>
> *And we are in:*

THE CLUB BERGHAIN, BERLIN

JIMMY *watches as* MONTE *inhales a line of cocaine. It blows his mind.*
JIMMY *turns to see the image of* EL GALLITO *in the mirror.*
The club music morphs into Schubert's 'Ave Maria', sung in either German or Spanish.
And we are in:

ACT TWO

HOTEL PARADISO, COROICO, BOLIVIA

ALVARO, *a Bolivian boy, is holding a tray of schnaps and three shot glasses. He wears the dirty shoes that* OLIVER *was wearing earlier.*

ALVARO *serves the drinks to* HEINRICH BARBIE, MONTE *and* JIMMY.

BARBIE: *Prost!*
MONTE: *Prost!*
JIMMY: *Prost!*

    BARBIE *refills their glasses.*

BARBIE: *Prost!*
MONTE: *Prost!*
JIMMY: *Prost!*

    BARBIE *refills their glasses.*

BARBIE: *Prost!*
MONTE: *Prost!*
JIMMY: *Prost!*
BARBIE: Welcome to Hotel Paradiso, Coroico.
MONTE: Thank you.
BARBIE: You enjoy the schnaps?
MONTE: *Ich liebe Schnaps.* [I love schnaps.]
BARBIE: *Ah, Sprechen Sie Deutsch?* [You speak German?]
MONTE: *Ein bisschen. Fünf Jahre auf dem Gymnasium und drei Monate feiern in Berlin Anfang der neunziger Jahre.* [A little. Five years at grammar school and three months partying in Berlin in the early 90s.]
BARBIE: *Dein Deutsch ist… ist… in ordnung.* [Your German is… is okay.]
MONTE: *Ah. Vielen Dank.* [Many thanks.]

    BARBIE *refills their glasses.*

BARBIE: *Prost!*
MONTE: *Prost!*
JIMMY: Pause?
BARBIE: *Was ist los mit deinem Freund?* [What is wrong with your friend?]
MONTE: Jimmy?
JIMMY: *Prost.*

JIMMY *drains the shot.*

MONTE: Herr Barbie—

BARBIE *halts the conversation to call attention to the music.*

BARBIE: Ah! Listen!

They listen.

Forgive me. Please. I am emotional. You like Schubert? / Yes?

JIMMY: Sherbet?

BARBIE & MONTE: [*together*] Schubert.

BARBIE: You know him?

MONTE: Of course.

BARBIE: He was Austrian, you know?

JIMMY: Australian?

BARBIE & MONTE: [*together*] Austrian.

BARBIE: This reminds me of my papa.

My papa gave to me a great love for the classical music.

He came here after the war like many of his countrymen.

First in Mexico but… he was not there long, no.

You know what they are saying about Mexico?

MONTE: What do they say?

BARBIE: So close to America so far from God.

So my father came here to Bolivia.

He saw opportunity.

He did very well in government in business.

He was a great man my papa.

A gentle man. *Ja.* A soft voice.

I remember as a child he would sing lullabies to send us off to dreamland.

BARBIE *sings a brief verse of a German lullaby.*

Guten Abend, gute Nacht, [Good evening, good night,]
mit Rosen bedacht, [Bedecked with roses,]
mit Näglein besteckt, [Adorned with carnations,]
schlupf unter die Deck: [Slip under the covers:]
Morgen früh, wenn Gott will, [Tomorrow morn, if God wills,]
wirst du wieder geweckt, [You'll awake once again,]

ACT TWO 37

> *morgen früh, wenn Gott will,* [Tomorrow morn, if God wills,] *wirst du wieder geweckt.* [You'll awake once again.]

JIMMY *only half listens to* BARBIE, *instead he tries to playfully distract* ALVARO.

You know I look like him, his twin.
One day I am at the airstrip in La Paz.
Many many years ago now.
I am waiting for a flight.
I am travelling on some business, I don't remember exactly…
Ah yes, yes I know, I am flying to Tijuana…
And so I am enjoying a beer and a cigar with my associates before the flight when a gentleman, a *Señor* approaches me.
He is maybe… fifty, sixty years old, he is well-dressed.
Yes. Okay.
This man he takes my coat you know like this…

BARBIE *grabs* JIMMY *roughly by the shirt.*

It's okay.
Now, we are in a bar. The second floor of the airport.
And this man he is pushing me against the railing, you know the edge, okay?
He is shouting at me in French.
In French he is saying, *'Meurtrier! Meurtier!'*
You speak French?
MONTE: *Un peu.* [A little.]
BARBIE: He is saying, 'You murdered my father, you murdered my mother!'
'You fucking Nazi!'
And all of this…

> *Pause.*

He is saying these things, shouting at me, and everyone in the bar they are afraid, you know, of what is going to happen.
This man, you know, he wants to kill me.
I know this because I see in his eyes.
This *Señor* he is serious.

Now, fortunately the *policia* arrive and they arrest this man. He would have killed me.
MONTE: You didn't know him?
BARBIE: I never saw him in my life.
It is only when I am on the aeroplane that I think.
Ah! *Ja*, I know.
I know what is this confusion.
> *Pause.*

He thought I was my father.
> BARBIE *fills their glasses.*

Now tomorrow you come to the *pelea de gallos*.
> BARBIE *strokes* ALVARO's *head.*

Alvaro here has a young cock he wishes to fight.
His name is Pablo, *ja*?
> ALVARO *nods.*

Have you been training Pablo the way I taught you?
> ALVARO *nods.*

You see you must first torture the cock and then you kiss it. And if it is wounded what you do? You piss on it. *Ja*? To purify it. In the *pelea* Señor Gallo is part of you. If you dies, a part of you dies too.
MONTE: I'm sorry, Herr Barbie, / but we…
BARBIE: Please call me Hienrich. We are friends now, *ja*?
MONTE: Hienrich, we have a flight leaving La Paz tomorrow night. I was expecting—
BARBIE: You come to Paradise for one day? All the way down El Camino de la Muerte?
No! No this this is a crime. You will stay. You are my guests. Relax. Swim. Eat. Drink. Anything you want. Wine. Beer. Schnaps. Sweets. Okay?
MONTE: Okay.
BARBIE: Okay.
MONTE: And our business, Hienrich, / when do we…?
BARBIE: *Ja ja*, we get to this… first you will see my champion cocks dance to the death.

JIMMY: Might give it a miss… go for a walk in the rainforest.

    BARBIE *pours another round of shots.*

BARBIE: You will come, both of you.

Okay?

MONTE: Okay.

    Beat.

JIMMY: Okay.

BARBIE: *Prost!*

MONTE: *Prost!*

    Beat.

JIMMY: *Prost.*

    And we are at:

THE IVY NIGHTCLUB, SYDNEY CBD

JIMMY *is dressed sharply in expensive new clothes. He stares at the mirrors in the men's bathroom. He is sweating.*

JIMMY *feels a wave of nausea and races into a cubicle.*

MONTE *enters, high on coke and booze.*

MONTE: [*singing*] Oh, Jimmy, you're so fine,

    You're so fine you blow my mind…

Hey, Jimmy.

Hey, Jimmy.

Hey, Jimmy?

JIMMY: Yuh.

MONTE: Jimmy?

JIMMY: Just a sec.

MONTE: Jimmy?

JIMMY: Just a sec.

    MONTE *bangs on the cubicle door.*

MONTE: It's the Gestapo, open the fuck up!

    JIMMY *emerges, holding his guts.*

        [*Singing*] You're so fine you blow my mind.

Hey, Jimmy.

> MONTE *shows* JIMMY *the bag of coke.*

You must try this Bolivian blow, it is pure as the driven snow.
JIMMY: I told you, / Monte.
MONTE: Come on, Jimmy, this is the real thing.

Always Coca-Cola.

Come on, Jimmy, one cap, one cap just for me, Jimmy, just for Monte.
JIMMY: I'm sick. I'm loosing my shit. Literally.
MONTE: This is medicine. Ask the Bolivians.

Ancient medicine from the Amazon.
JIMMY: They say it turns white men into fuckwits.
MONTE: Who says?
JIMMY: Bolivian curse.
MONTE: Where'd you hear that?
JIMMY: Lonely Planet.
MONTE: Well fuck Lonely Planet.

Fuck the Bolivians.

And fuck their funny felt hats.

> MONTE *aeroplanes the cap of coke towards* JIMMY*'s nose.*
>
> EL GALLITO *enters the bathroom. He goes to the urinals.*
>
> JIMMY *is hyper-aware of* EL GALLITO*'s presence, but* MONTE *ignores him.*

This is how I used to get Oli to eat his kale.
Here we go… here we go, it's come all this way on a big, big aeroplane.
Over the hills over the dales over the oceans wide.
Uh-oh.
The plane is out of fuel… Uh-oh, the plane needs to land.
Open up, little prince.
Open up…
Up…
Up…

> JIMMY *stands his ground.* MONTE *gives up the game.*

You are officially a Party Pooper.

ACT TWO

>EL GALLITO *stands beside* JIMMY, *facing the mirror.*
>
>JIMMY *turns to look at him.*
>
>EL GALLITO *leaves without looking at* JIMMY.

JIMMY: I'm off.
MONTE: No you're not.
>We're celebrating.
>One down safe and sound, next one on its way.
>We are up up and away, Jimmy.

JIMMY: Yeah, next time.
MONTE: Step into my office.
>Tell Monte.
>What's eating you?
>
>>JIMMY *looks out after* EL GALLITO.

JIMMY: How come I'm still pushing in Penrith?
>Blow so cut you could bake a cake with it.

MONTE: Hey, a pinch of gluten free flour never hurt anyone. Least I'm looking out for the coeliacs.
JIMMY: Yeah, you tell that to all the brickies.
MONTE: Come on, Jimmy. Goon might as well be Moet. Coon, camembert. Bogans don't have the nose to tell the difference.
JIMMY: Why don't I cover the Inner West?
MONTE: You wanna be a hipster barista?
>You'll have to grow some facial hair to fit in there, Jimmy.

JIMMY: How come Christos gets the penthouse in Darlinghurst and I'm in a shit one-bedroom sixpack?
MONTE: Hey, your sister bought you that. I had nothing to do with it.
JIMMY: I'm on the line.
MONTE: Yeah?
JIMMY: I'm the cunt still pimping La Madre's shit coke.
MONTE: I told you I'll set you up.
JIMMY: What about Bolivia?
MONTE: What did I say?
JIMMY: What we did.
MONTE: You Jimmy. What you did.

>*Beat.*

JIMMY: When do I get remunerated?
MONTE: How long have you been working for me, Jimmy?
JIMMY: I dunno—
MONTE: How long?
JIMMY: Six months.
MONTE: Blink of an eye. [*Pause.*] You're dismissed.

> JIMMY *goes to leave,* MONTE *grabs him.*

> Wait. [*Pause.*] Give us a hug.

>> JIMMY *and* MONTE *hug.*

> They're nice.

JIMMY: What?
MONTE: Shoes.

> And the jacket…

> That's not…

>> MONTE *checks the label.*

> It is.

> You come into some money, Jimmy?

JIMMY: Well yeah, I –
MONTE: It's okay. Relax.

> You look hot. Just like your sister.

> She's looking out for you, you know.

JIMMY: I know.
MONTE: This is where we met.
JIMMY: Yeah.
MONTE: Have I told you the story, / Jimmy?
JIMMY: You tell it all the time, Monte.
MONTE: It's a great / story.
JIMMY: / Yeah no it's not.
MONTE: Scarlet loves it.
JIMMY: She doesn't / if you actually asked her….
MONTE: Did you see those Estonian twin models at the bar?

> Eurovision they are.

> I could have them.

> I could have both of them. / Simulfuckingtaneously.

ACT TWO

JIMMY: Sure, Monte.
MONTE: But I won't because I have Scarlet.
 I have your sister from scabby Cabramatta / and—
JIMMY: Okay, Monte…
MONTE: —we are living the dream.
JIMMY: I'm happy for you.
MONTE: Where would she be without me? Hey?
 You know. I know.
 Can't hide where you're from.
 You can wear your Tommy Hilfiger jacket and your… your what brand are those…?

> MONTE *grabs* JIMMY'*s chinos.*

 What brand are they?
JIMMY: Maison Martin.
MONTE: Maison Martin chinos and your Ralph Lauren fucking… what are they…?
JIMMY: Calf-skin loafers.
MONTE: Calf-skin fucking loafers, but when you rock up at Portsea Polo with me, Jimmy, Jimmy you'll always look just that teeny bit like a turd on an hors d'oeuvre.
JIMMY: I'm off.
MONTE: I've got some advice for you, Jimmy. Here's some toilet paper, take some fucking notes. Man was not created equal. There's a pecking order. If you want to thrive in this world you've got to fuck the cunts below and lick the cunts above.

> *Pause.*

JIMMY: Is that it, Monte?

> *Pause.*

MONTE: Do you have a cock?
JIMMY: What?
MONTE: A cock, Jimmy, do you have a cock?
JIMMY: I'm calling you a cab, Monte. / You should go home to your…

> JIMMY *pulls out his phone.*

MONTE: Are you calling me a cock?

You're a cock.
You're a cock.

> MONTE *grabs at* JIMMY*'s cock.*

JIMMY: What are you doing?
MONTE: Just checking.
JIMMY: Fucking hell, Monte.

> MONTE *forces* JIMMY *into a headlock.*

/ Monte, let go… Monte… please… let go… Monte… Monte…
MONTE: Hey hey hey don't struggle don't struggle don't struggle I won't hurt you if don't struggle don't struggle… bro… bro… bro… bro… bro… bro…

> JIMMY *stops struggling.*

There we go.
    [*Singing*] It's guys like you, Jimmy…
    … don't break my heart, Jimmy…
    I went to boarding school…
    … I did woodwork.
JIMMY: Monte.
MONTE: [*singing*] I'm the king…
    … and you're the… I'm the king.
JIMMY: Okay…okay.

> MONTE *kisses* JIMMY *quickly on the lips before letting him go.*

> MONTE *sets up another line of coke.*

MONTE: Now how do you say, 'Suck my cock', in Estonian?
Jimmy?

> JIMMY *stares coldly at* MONTE *as he inhales another line.*

Never mind. I'll google it.

And we are:

IN THE STREET OUTSIDE THE IVY

JIMMY *hails a cab.*
Behind him, EL GALLITO *leans against a wall. He's staring at* JIMMY.

EL GALLITO: *¿Hey, cabrón, dónde está tu fierro?* [Hey, gangster, where's your gun?]

    JIMMY *turns around slowly.*

JIMMY: Are you talking to me?

    And we are:

IN DARKNESS

We hear…

EL GALLITO: *Santísima Muerte,*
    Señora de la noche,
    Señora de los destinos.
    En este día me acerco a ti para pedirte,
    Suplicarte oigas mis quejas.

    Señora, madre mía,
    Para tu mano justiciera
    No existen imposibles.

    Tu tienes el dominio
    Sobre la vida y la muerte,
    Que esta familia
    No tenga reposo,
    Ni en cuerpo ni en espíritu
    Así sea.

END OF ACT TWO

ACT THREE

And we are in:

JIMMY'S APARTMENT, PENRITH

Night.

JIMMY *enters with six Cokes in a plastic IGA bag and a pizza box.*

JIMMY *takes a can from the bag and opens it.*

He places it on the table.

JIMMY: *Uno.*

>JIMMY *opens another can and begins a row of six.*

Dos.

>*He opens another and another and another.*

Tres.

Cuatro.

Cinco.

Seis.

>JIMMY *stands back.*

>EL GALLITO *enters the room wearing* JIMMY*'s shirt.*

>*He takes a Coke and drinks it.*

>JIMMY *goes to kiss* EL GALLITO.

>EL GALLITO *finds Grubbe's business card in* JIMMY*'s shirt. He flicks it at* JIMMY. JIMMY *swipes it and slips it into his back pocket.*

You know what I'd like to do? You know what I would like to do most in the whole fucking world? I would like to take you shopping. I would like to buy you anything you want. I'd like to dress you. I would like to take you somewhere, buy you a really nice fucking suit. Two suits. No, a week of suits. A Monday to Sunday of really nice fucking suits. Sharp really well-cut. And shoes. A really nice pair of shoes, yeah? Like these? Do you like these? These are veau

ACT THREE

velour. They're really fucking soft. You don't get softer leather than veau velour. They're made from calf. That's why they cost a packet. They're slaughtered before they get the chance to grow up. Which is shit, which is really fucking horrible but actually, I really don't care because look how good they look? What do you say? Are you in? I got a hook-up in the morning but after let's go shopping.

> EL GALLITO *finishes his Coke.*
>
> JIMMY *kisses* EL GALLITO *again.*
>
> EL GALLITO *kisses him back then bites him on the lip.*
>
> JIMMY*'s lip bleeds.*
>
> EL GALLITO *grins.*
>
> *And we are in:*

GUZMAN Y GOMEZ, BONDI JUNCTION

GRUBBE *enters and drops a burrito in front of* JIMMY.

GRUBBE: One bean burrito. Sour cream guacamole extra *jalapeños*.

> JIMMY *consumes it ravenously.*

Over the gastro?
JIMMY: Yeah, I'm empty.
GRUBBE: Well fill up Jimmy you're a growing boy.
JIMMY: I'm ready to negotiate.
GRUBBE: Good to see you've got your colour back.
JIMMY: First up I'm keeping my assets.
GRUBBE: Such as?
JIMMY: My property.
GRUBBE: You're a man of property, Jimmy?
JIMMY: I own a flat in Penrith.
GRUBBE: Explain to me how you entered the Sydney property market on Newstart allowance?
JIMMY: It was a present.
GRUBBE: In Penrith that was generous. You get the first home buyer bonus?
JIMMY: Yep.

GRUBBE: I love this country.
JIMMY: Got a car too.
GRUBBE: You're a real grown-up.
JIMMY: It's a Mazda.
GRUBBE: Yeah, what year?
JIMMY: 2002.
GRUBBE: So Monte Silverthorn of 39 Windsor Street Woollahra, born with a silver spoon up his arse, gives you a 2002 Mazda while he cruises round in a brand-new Benz. Sounds like you've been taking most of the risk without any of the fringe benefits. I guess that's why you're here, is it?
JIMMY: Monte never set me up.
GRUBBE: Who did?
JIMMY: Scarlet. My / sister?
GRUBBE: Monte's money.
JIMMY: It's in her name, it's all in trust.
>   *Beat.*

GRUBBE: Monte's not just a pretty face.
JIMMY: Scarlet saved my skin. Kept me out of prison.
GRUBBE: I know. Three-year suspended sentence, twelve months parole. Those charges: you must've got the judge on his birthday.
JIMMY: Scarlet made Monte vouch for me. Him and his family.
GRUBBE: The Silverthorns throw a lot of weight. All legit these days but you can trace the Silverthorns right back to the First Fleet and they weren't shipped out here for nicking a loaf of bread. Does she know?
JIMMY: What?
GRUBBE: You've been pimping parrot in Penrith Plaza?
JIMMY: —
GRUBBE: She'll find out sooner or later.
JIMMY: Monte's a prick.
GRUBBE: Really?
JIMMY: She's better off without him.
GRUBBE: She might not see it like that.
    Not so comfortable slipping rank.
JIMMY: She won't have to.
GRUBBE: How you figure that?

ACT THREE

Beat.

JIMMY: I keep everything I've earned.
GRUBBE: You've been on the dole for ten years, you've never submitted a tax return.
JIMMY: What I've saved then.
GRUBBE: Where'd you make the deposit? Hole in the bush?
JIMMY: Something like that.
GRUBBE: Tell you what, dig it up bring it in and if you're very good you'll get to keep a third of it.
JIMMY: All of it.
GRUBBE: Half of it. If you can prove it's profit from gambling.
JIMMY: Don't gamble.
GRUBBE: I recommend you take it up. If it looks like you've financially gained from a deal with us the defence will argue your evidence is tainted, motivated by greed.
That wouldn't be true would it Jimmy?
JIMMY: Never.
GRUBBE: Look, I understand. You're thinking of the future. You've got your eyes on the road ahead. So have I. I retire in a couple of months. You know they're saying you'll need one point six five million in your super fund, that's if you retire at the age of sixty-five. That'll last just about until you're ninety-one which these days is a foreseeable age, barring a U.V.E.
JIMMY: A what?
GRUBBE: Unforseen Violent Event.

Pause.

JIMMY: I want protection.
GRUBBE: I'm sure we can sort something out.
JIMMY: Full witness protection. Me, my sister, her kid.
GRUBBE: Immediate family only Jimmy.
JIMMY: Protection for them or no deal.
GRUBBE: Who do you think we are, Ronald McDonald House? Witness protection program is funded by taxpayer money, people like me who've worked their whole lives.
JIMMY: Fuck it then.

JIMMY screws up his taco wrappers and goes to leave.

GRUBBE: How long do you think you'd last inside?
They will consume you. You know what I mean. Then what will your sister and nephew do?
JIMMY: I'm giving you a major player.
GRUBBE: You're not.
JIMMY: Monte's big now.
GRUBBE: He's a sardine in the scheme of things.
JIMMY: So why bust a gut old man?
GRUBBE: Down at the A.C.C. in Surry we have an index of organised crime figures.
You Jimmy Jones are right down the bottom.
We call it the scum layer.
Monte? He's somewhere in the low middle and La Madre she's right there up the top.
So, we're using a little fish—
JIMMY: Me.
GRUBBE: —to snag a middle-sized fish—
JIMMY: Monte.
GRUBBE: —to harpoon the great white whale.
JIMMY: La Madre.
GRUBBE: You got it.
JIMMY: I'm bait.
GRUBBE: Bait that might just get off the hook if it plays its role right.
JIMMY: If you're retiring—
GRUBBE: Three months one week two days.
JIMMY: —why go after La Madre?
GRUBBE: I had a daughter. She'd be about your age. She hated my guts growing up. I was never there, always on the job. What is it with kids these days, they look at you like you've committed some terrible crime. The whole time they're growing up you're trying to grease them. Maybe we have, maybe we have committed a crime, we just can't remember what it was. I bought her a horse. Every little girl wants a pony. I'm just a constable at the time, earning piss-all and I buy my daughter a pony like she was a princess. I needed my head read. It's not just the pony, it's all the paraphernalia that goes with it, you know the saddle, the helmet, the lessons. I thought it'd make her

happy. But the more you get the more you want. Don't you, Jimmy? Did I cop shit down at the shop? They joked I was grass-feeding, that I paid for that little gelding in bribes. I didn't. I never have. Not so much as a free Macca. I'd shake my head, count out the silver, down to the last five fucking cents. I think I deserve a trophy for all that. A trophy with a big fucking cock on it because there's no justice with scum like you doing deals with the A.C.C. walking away scot-free with a retirement package three times the size of mine.

No, there's no such thing as fucking justice.

JIMMY: You need me.
GRUBBE: Plenty more fish in the sea.
JIMMY: No-one as close to Monte.
GRUBBE: —
JIMMY: Full police protection. The three of us.

New IDs, new CVs.
GRUBBE: You have a current CV do you Jimmy?

What's on it?

Six years as a full-time meth head and a half-finished TAFE course?

That'll knock the socks of your new employer.
JIMMY: Deal or La Madre's the one that gets away.
GRUBBE: Did you just grow an inch?

JIMMY *smiles.*

You're happy to retire are you Jimmy?
JIMMY: Sure.
GRUBBE: At the ripe old age of twenty-five, you'll give up the game?
JIMMY: Depends if my deal's sweet enough.
GRUBBE: Too sweet it'll rot your teeth.
JIMMY: I'll buy new ones.

So you send us overseas, okay. Somewhere nice.
GRUBBE: Nice enough.
JIMMY: Ibiza.
GRUBBE: Echuca.
JIMMY: Berlin.
GRUBBE: Brisbane.
JIMMY: Zurich.

GRUBBE: New Zealand.
>   *Beat.*

JIMMY: Five-star accommodation.
GRUBBE: Three.
JIMMY: Five.
GRUBBE: Three and a half.
JIMMY: Five.
> And a new BMW.

GRUBBE: Don't push your fucking luck.
JIMMY: How bad do you want La Madre?
GRUBBE: You're getting cocky Jimmy. I'd keep an eye on that.
>   *Pause.*

JIMMY: When do we do it?
GRUBBE: Couple of weeks.
JIMMY: Why so long?
GRUBBE: There's a process.
> Forms to fill out, memorandums to sign, psychological assessments.

JIMMY: Psych tests?
GRUBBE: Is that going to be a problem?
JIMMY: Nuh.
GRUBBE: Clean aren't you?
JIMMY: Yeah.
GRUBBE: You're out of the program if you're using.
JIMMY: I'm clean.
GRUBBE: We need to establish you're of sound mind and body or your evidence will be inadmissible in a court of law.
JIMMY: Yeah I got it.
GRUBBE: If that happens you're on your own.
> No protection, no deal.
> I don't care about your welfare Jimmy. You're fish flakes.

JIMMY: Don't you have a partner? Where's the good cop? I want to talk to him for a change 'cause you're a real prick.
GRUBBE: I'm like Pert. You know Pert, the two-in-one shampoo conditioner? I'm good cop bad cop in one convenient container.
JIMMY: Hate Pert, doesn't work.
GRUBBE: Tough luck, I'm all you got.

ACT THREE

JIMMY: What now?
GRUBBE: You get me some evidence.
JIMMY: Like what?
GRUBBE: Monte's hidey hole.

Where's he stashing the snow?

JIMMY: I dunno.
GRUBBE: Storage unit, spare apartment… What about his house?
JIMMY: He's not retarded.
GRUBBE: Yacht, safety deposit box…
JIMMY: He doesn't tell me that shit.
GRUBBE: Well have a sticky beak in his laptop and fucking find out.

JIMMY seems daunted by this.

You're on the right road.

Keep going, don't look down, don't look back.

If you start to doubt that, have a squiz at this.

GRUBBE pushes the envelope across the table.

JIMMY: What is it?
GRUBBE: —

JIMMY opens the envelope. He sees crime scene photographs of Christos's dismembered body.

Christos Lymbious. Washed up on Maroubra beach this morning sans scrotum.

JIMMY: Sans…? Oh fuck.
GRUBBE: That's a Columbian necktie. What you do is you slash the throat like so and pull the tongue out through the slit.

I imagine it's quite difficult. I've never been able to master the Windsor.

JIMMY: Oh fuck oh fuck oh fuck.
GRUBBE: Looks like La Madre's got wind Monte's been importing The Butcher's coke.
JIMMY: You know about The Butcher?
GRUBBE: Open your eyes, Jimmy.
JIMMY: They're open.
GRUBBE: You certain about that?

I hope you've got something to sling if La Madre's amigos come for you too.

JIMMY *shakes his head.*

I tell you what.

GRUBBE *writes a number on the back of a Guzman y Gomez serviette.*

Here's the number of a bloke I know in Fairy Meadow.

I'd give him a bell otherwise you could be sporting a second smile.

GRUBBE *leaves* JIMMY *with the photographs.*

And we are in:

MONTE AND SCARLET'S HOUSE

JIMMY *is drinking Coke and searching Monte's laptop computer.*

OLIVER *enters from the darkness, wearing pyjamas and a dirty Bolivian beanie. He is sick and has a fever. He draws the toy gun from his pyjamas and points it at* JIMMY.

JIMMY *starts when he sees* OLIVER *and slams the laptop shut.*

JIMMY: You're awake.
OLIVER: —
JIMMY: You're supposed to be in bed.
OLIVER: —
JIMMY: Asleep.
OLIVER: —
JIMMY: Are you sick?

JIMMY *notices* OLIVER'S *beanie.*

Did your dad bring you that back from overseas?

OLIVER *looks at the computer.*

OLIVER: That's Daddy's laptop.
JIMMY: Want some Coke?
OLIVER: —
JIMMY: You like Coke don't you?

OLIVER *nods.*

Want some or not?

OLIVER *nods.*

ACT THREE

    JIMMY *gives* OLIVER *a can.*

Our secret.

    JIMMY *watches* OLIVER *drink.*

    JIMMY *takes it away from* OLIVER.

That's enough.
OLIVER: This isn't your house.
JIMMY: Cheers for pointing that out.
OLIVER: One day I'll get everything.
JIMMY: Really holding out for that aren't you?
OLIVER: I'm a prince you're just a knight.
JIMMY: What about the new baby?

When it's born you'll have to share.
Your parents will be bored with you.
Yeah.
You know how your mum bought a new plasma screen last week even though there was nothing wrong with the old one?
It's the same with children.
The new one gets all the attention and the old one's sold on eBay.
Or worse, it's dumped on the street.

    OLIVER *considers this.*

So in the future you and I should stick together.

    Pause.

Give us a look at that beanie Oli.
OLIVER: I had a night terror.
JIMMY: That sounds scary.
OLIVER: The Little Rooster came.
JIMMY: Who's The Little Rooster?
OLIVER: —
JIMMY: Why do you call him that?
OLIVER: —
JIMMY: What does The Little Rooster do?
OLIVER: Wakes me up.
JIMMY: Why?
OLIVER: He wants to play a game.

JIMMY: What game?

OLIVER: *Quietos*.

JIMMY: How do you play it?

OLIVER: You shoot your enemies and they have to freeze.
I'll show you.

> *OLIVER shoots JIMMY with his replica gun.*

Freeze!
You're dead.
You have to die.
Die.

> *JIMMY does nothing.*

You have to die now Uncle Jimmy.
Die die die die die die die die die…

> *JIMMY chases OLIVER and shakes him violently.*

/ die die die die die die die die die.

JIMMY: Hey.
Hey.
Hey.
Stop.

> *There is real menace in this moment, as if JIMMY is about to strangle OLIVER.*

OLIVER: *Señor, no se olvide que soy delicado.* [Don't forget that I am soft.]

> *JIMMY releases OLIVER.*

> *OLIVER runs away.*

> *JIMMY is left holding the toy gun. He looks at it. He slips the gun into his jacket sleeve.*

JIMMY: I'm standing here.
You make the move.

> *And we are in:*

ACT THREE

JIMMY'S APARTMENT, PENRITH

JIMMY *performs a very broken-down version of Bickle's routine in Scorcese's* Taxi Driver. *The physicality of the moment is more important than the language here.*

JIMMY: You talking to me… [*etc.*]

    EL GALLITO *appears behind* JIMMY *and bites him on the neck.*

MONTE: Well?

    EL GALLITO *leaves as* JIMMY *swings around to* MONTE.

And we are in:

MONTE AND SCARLET'S HOUSE

JIMMY *tucks the gun into the back of his jeans and lifts his collar to hide the bite.*

JIMMY: He's not there.
MONTE: You talk to his mum?
JIMMY: Yeah.
MONTE: And?

    Pause.

JIMMY: He hasn't been home for a few days.
MONTE: And the bag?

    JIMMY *is looking at the rooster drawing on the wall.*

JIMMY: What's this?
MONTE: The bag Jimmy—
JIMMY: ?
MONTE: —from the airport, the bag Christos picked up?
JIMMY: Not there.
MONTE: You had a thorough look did you?
JIMMY: Yeah.
MONTE: Yes?
JIMMY: Yes.
MONTE: You look under the old woman's bed?

JIMMY: What? No.

    MONTE *dials Christos's number.*

MONTE: Why not?

    That's where'd I'd be hiding twenty keys of pure-grade cocaine, I would be hiding it under—

    SCARLET *enters with a Spray n' Wipe.*

    —a stroke victim's mattress.

    SCARLET *has heard this.*

SCARLET: Are you calling the cleaner Monte?

    Beat.

MONTE: I am baby. [*To* JIMMY] No answer.
SCARLET: If Alma's not there call Juana.
MONTE: Juana the Iguana. Got it.
SCARLET: Tell her it's urgent.

    SCARLET *sprays the drawing on the wall. The stain remains.*

MONTE: [*to* JIMMY] Let's go for a stroll.
SCARLET: What do you think of the new wall art, Jimmy?
MONTE: Baby?
SCARLET: Oliver draws them every night.
MONTE: Let the cleaner take care of it.
SCARLET: He's been vomiting, Jimmy, running a fever. You must have brought it back from wherever the fuck you came from.

    Where was that again?

    JIMMY *looks at* MONTE.

JIMMY: Berlin.
SCARLET: Berlin.

    He's been waking up when we're asleep but he doesn't call out, he doesn't come in to us.

    He draws these.

    What do you think that is / Jimmy?

    JIMMY *shrugs.*

    He says it's a rooster.

MONTE: Confiscate the crayons.

ACT THREE

SCARLET: This is lipstick.
MONTE: He's an artist.
SCARLET: He's sick Monte.
MONTE: Creative delirium.

> SCARLET *shows* JIMMY *an empty Coca-Cola can.*

SCARLET: You don't know anything about this do you Jimmy? Found it in his room.
JIMMY: No.
SCARLET: You drink Coke / so—
JIMMY: Now and then.
SCARLET: Did you give one to Oli?
JIMMY: No, when?
SCARLET: The other night when we went out when you looked after him did you give him a Coke?
JIMMY: No.
SCARLET: Do you know what coke does? Apart from burning holes in the mucous membrane of their stomachs the body ups its dopamine production stimulating the pleasure centre of the brain.
JIMMY: Right.
SCARLET: They get high Jimmy. Just like smack. You know all about that.
MONTE: Baby don't you have a lunch date?
SCARLET: Might explain why he's drawing pictures like this, waking up in the middle of the night half out of his mind.
JIMMY: I didn't give him the Coke Scarlet.

> SCARLET *stares at* JIMMY.

SCARLET: Oliver? Can you come here please?

> OLIVER *enters in his pyjamas. He's wearing Alvaro's shoes, beanie and jumper.*
>
> *He is deathly pale and his hands are covered in red.*
>
> JIMMY *takes a step back.*

Where'd you get the Coke, Oli?
Tell Mummy.

> OLIVER *slowly points his red finger at the picture of the rooster on the wall.*

The rooster gave it to you did he?

Pause.

No more cola, Oli.

Okay?

It's not good for sick boys.

SCARLET *whips out some wet wipes to clean* OLIVER*'s hands.*

Now come here, I want to clean you up.

OLIVER *submits to the process.*

SCARLET *gets some red on her white dress.*

Fuck.

Oli come with me to the bathroom.

SCARLET *and* OLIVER *leave.*

MONTE: So where's Christos?

Is he: a) at a Narcotics Anonymous weekend retreat; b) on a P&O cruise on his way to the Greek Islands; c) lost in a time/space continuum; or d) down the Gold Coast blowing twenty keys of pure Bolivian blow up his hairy nose?

Lock in D, Eddy.

JIMMY: Or F.

Beat.

MONTE: There is no F.

MONTE *stares at* JIMMY.

Do you have a theory Jimmy?

JIMMY: Yeah no I dunno.

Pause.

MONTE: One more.
JIMMY: What?
MONTE: One more pick-up.
JIMMY: From La Madre?
MONTE: I got a call.
JIMMY: You told The Butcher—
MONTE: Three, and that's it.

ACT THREE

JIMMY: —we were done with La Madre.
MONTE: Think about it—
JIMMY: No.
MONTE: —we don't pick up—
JIMMY: No way.
MONTE: —it smells off.
BRATISLAV: This one.

> JIMMY *turns to see* BRATISLAV *pointing out cardboard Storage King boxes.*

JIMMY: I can't.
MONTE: Do you know something I don't?
JIMMY: No.

> *And we are in:*

A WAREHOUSE, ST PETERS

BRATISLAV: This one.
This one.

> JIMMY *stacks the boxes onto a trolley.* BRATISLAV *watches him.*

JIMMY: Out of interest Bratislav… how did you get into the gravestone-making business? Because it's not a career that springs to mind, that springs to a young person's mind when they're thinking what is it that I want to be when I grow up? How do I want to make my mark?

> JIMMY *jumps as* BRATISLAV *receives a call on his mobile.*

BRATISLAV: *Zdravo?* [Hello?]
Eh?

> BRATISLAV *listens. He hangs up.*
> JIMMY *places the last box on the trolley and goes to wheel it away.*

Wait.

> BRATISLAV *exits.*

JIMMY: Everything okay?
Bratislav?

> JIMMY *touches his shirt sleeve to check his gun is still there.*

BRATISLAV *returns with another box.*

BRATISLAV: This one.

    BRATISLAV *places the box on the trolley.*

JIMMY: I was told there were three.

BRATISLAV: *Četiri.* [Four.]

    Pause.

JIMMY: Yeah, I'm pretty sure it was just three.

BRATISLAV: I am gravestone maker because my father was gravestone maker and his father and his father and his father for a thousand fucking years of fathers. Then there is war and there's no time for gravestone making. Too busy killing. Too many dead. So we bulldoze bodies into great big fucking pits, maybe field, forest, foundations for shopping centre, something like this. No grave, no mark, no memory, no fucking nothing. In war everything is fucked.

Wife.

Lover.

Sister.

Nephew.

Message from La Madre.

    MONTE *stares at the four boxes.*

MONTE: There's four.

BRATISLAV: You tell that *drkadžija* you work for to look behind him, because we bring the ways of the old world to your sunny fucking shores.

MONTE: Why are there four here Jimmy?

JIMMY: That's what he gave me.

MONTE: We agreed on three.

JIMMY: That's what I told him.

    BRATISLAV *faces up to* JIMMY, *directing this last threat at him before exiting.*

BRATISLAV: May your mother recognise you in meat pie.

    And we are in:

ACT THREE

A STORAGE UNIT, POTTS POINT

MONTE *hands a box cutter to* JIMMY.

MONTE: Open them.
JIMMY: Me?
MONTE: Don't fuck about.

> JIMMY *cuts into the box. It's full of packaged cocaine.*

Next one.

> JIMMY *cuts into the second and the third box. They both contain cocaine.*

JIMMY: Monte I / don't—
MONTE: Just do it.

> JIMMY *cuts into the last box.*
>
> *It takes* JIMMY *a few seconds to register what he's looking at.*
>
> JIMMY *steps back and dry wretches.*
>
> MONTE *takes a look.*

JIMMY: Christos.
MONTE: Hard to tell.
  It's not circumcised.

> MONTE *thinks.*

GRUBBE: Eat your pho, Jimmy.

> JIMMY *turns to see* GRUBBE *sitting at a table with a bowl of steaming pho.*

MONTE: Bring the car round.
JIMMY: No—
MONTE: Bring the car around.
JIMMY: —I can't do this.
MONTE & GRUBBE: [*together*] Yes you can.
JIMMY: No.
MONTE: Take La Madre's coke to this address. Storage King, St Leonards. Six, one, eight, four.
JIMMY: What's that?
MONTE: Pin code, Jimmy, got it?

JIMMY: Yeah.
MONTE: Repeat it.
JIMMY: Six, one, eight, four.
MONTE: Don't forget.
JIMMY: What about—?
MONTE: Take a drive out to Botany Bay, toss it.
JIMMY: In the water?
MONTE: Where do you think?
GRUBBE: Eat your pho, Jimmy.
JIMMY: Who's next?
MONTE: You if you don't get your skates on.
JIMMY: What if—?
MONTE: Just do it.

And we are in:

A VIETNAMESE RESTRAUNT, CABRAMATTA

GRUBBE: This is the best pho in Sydney. Everything's fresh, grown local. Now the decor's not hipster and I admit there's a trace of mouse shit under the placemats, but since the health inspector shut it down last year it's really cleaned up its act.
JIMMY: I feel sick.
GRUBBE: Pinochet reared his fascist head?
JIMMY: ?
GRUBBE: The bug back?
Told you it doesn't go away. It lives in your stomach until you kill it. This'll fix you up. Like medicine this stuff, hell of a lot healthier than a Krispy Kreme donut. Do I have to play aeroplanes? Here we go.

GRUBBE flies the soup spoon towards JIMMY.

Open up.

JIMMY swallows.

How's that?
Told you, best fucking pho in the city.
Have another go.

JIMMY scoops another spoonful from the bowl.

Pho pin xe lua.

Bull's penis soup.
See that hole there in the meat?
That's the urethra.

> JIMMY *wretches.*

Now what have you got for me Jimmy?

> JIMMY *puts the box on the table.*

What's this?

JIMMY: Have a 'squiz'.

> GRUBBE *opens the box, looks in.*

Thought you'd like to put it with the rest of him. Sew it back on or something.

GRUBBE: Well that's very thoughtful of you Jimmy, his mother'll be touched, but where's Monte storing his gear?

JIMMY: How'd they know?

How'd they know when Christos was doing the pick-up?

GRUBBE: Oh well small town word gets around.

JIMMY: No-one else knew but you.

GRUBBE: And you Jimmy.

You knew.

> *Pause.*

JIMMY: I told La Madre?

GRUBBE: Didn't you?

JIMMY: Why the fuck would I tell La Madre?

GRUBBE: Think about it.

> JIMMY *seriously considers this for a moment.*

JIMMY: No no you did this you let this leak. You let this happen to Christos.

GRUBBE: Your brother-in-law started this when he chose to shake hands with a Nazi.

You know, South America was crawling with Nazis after the war. Barbie's father Klaus was a nasty piece of work. He'd play Schubert on the piano while his prisoners were tortured to death.

That's why they called him The Butcher. Sounds like his son liked the name so much he inherited it.

Later Barbie gained popularity with the C.I.A. for helping to hunt down Che Guevara in the jungles of Bolivia. They riddled him with bullets and lay his bloodied body on a cement slab in a school with a dirt floor. They even dressed him in new clothes and gave him a nice new haircut. You might wonder what Che was thinking when he tried to take on the big cocks. Well like everyone, Jimmy, Che Guevara had a dose of *mortido*.

JIMMY: What if I don't do this?
GRUBBE: You've signed the memorandum Jimmy.
JIMMY: Maybe I want out.
GRUBBE: There is no out.
You're up to your neck in this.
There are tales from the old days of Mexico that'd drain your blood.
Make no mistake, The Butcher and La Madre are not great mates.
There's a reason why in three decades I haven't been able to come within an inch of La Madre.
JIMMY: You're a shithouse detective?

GRUBBE *slaps* JIMMY *around the ear.*

GRUBBE: No-one's ever had the guts to fuck with her.
Monte in his coked-up ignorance has.
He's put you and your family at risk.
By rolling you protect them.
Them and your assets.
Where's the gear?

JIMMY *hesitates, then writes down an address on a serviette.*

JIMMY: It's here.
GRUBBE: Sure about that?
JIMMY: I put it there.

GRUBBE *goes to leave.*

GRUBBE: You wanted this.
JIMMY: What?
GRUBBE: Yeah you've been dreaming this.
JIMMY: —
GRUBBE: *Öffne deine Augen.* [Open your eyes.]

ACT THREE

> JIMMY *is suddenly awake as if from a nightmare.*
>
> *And we are in:*

JIMMY'S APARTMENT, NIGHT

EL GALLITO *is asleep in the bed beside* JIMMY.

JIMMY *picks up a pillow and goes to smother* EL GALLITO.

EL GALLITO *is suddenly awake.*

EL GALLITO: *Almohada.* [Pillow.]
JIMMY: *¿Qué?* [What?]
EL GALLITO: *Almohada.* [Pillow.]
JIMMY: *Almohada.* [Pillow.]

> JIMMY *takes* EL GALLITO'*s lifeless hand and animates it.*

EL GALLITO: *Mano.* [Hand.]
JIMMY: *Mano.* [Hand.]

> JIMMY *picks up a Coke can.*

Coca-Cola.

Easy.

> JIMMY *points at the various body parts. He repeats the Spanish words after* EL GALLITO.

EL GALLITO: *Labios.* [Lips.]

Ojos. [Eyes.]

Corazón. [Heart.]

Estómago. [Stomach.]

> JIMMY *traces a scar across* EL GALLITO'*s abdomen.*

JIMMY: Scar?
EL GALLITO: *Cicatriz.* [Scar.]
JIMMY: *Cicatriz.* [Scar.]

> JIMMY *goes to kiss* EL GALLITO.

EL GALLITO: *Cierra tus ojos.* [Close your eyes.]

> EL GALLITO *closes* JIMMY'*s eyelids.*

Cierralos. [Close them.]

JIMMY *resists.*

Duerme. [Sleep.]
JIMMY: No.
EL GALLITO: *¿Qué te pasa?* [What's bugging you?]

JIMMY *leaves the bed, paces the apartment. He's agitated. He checks doors, windows.*

Conozco tus pesadillas. [I know your nightmares.]
JIMMY: *¿Que?* [What?]

EL GALLITO *reaches for a cigarette. He lights it and shares it with* JIMMY.

Have you seen a dead body?
EL GALLITO: —
JIMMY: Corpse? *Un muerto?* / Have you smelt it?
EL GALLITO: *¿Y tu?* [Have you?]
JIMMY: This kid I knew.
We used together.
One morning I woke up.
It was early, still dark.
He was cold.
His / mouth…
EL GALLITO: … *boca…* [… mouth…]
JIMMY: … his…
EL GALLITO: … *labios…* [… lips…]
JIMMY: … were…
EL GALLITO: … *azules.* [… blue.]
JIMMY: He'd choked.
Choked on his…
EL GALLITO: … *vomito.* [… vomit.]
JIMMY: I was sleeping. I was asleep.
EL GALLITO: … *dormido.* [… asleep.]
JIMMY: I washed him.
Every part inside out.
Combed his hair, shaved him, brushed his teeth.
I dressed him.

ACT THREE

Jeans.
Socks.
Shoes.
Then I lay next to him.
And I waited for, the sun, for morning,
for him to wake up.

> JIMMY *is crying.*

I loved—

> EL GALLITO *laughs.*

> JIMMY *fires with rage.*

EL GALLITO: *Ese eras tu.* [That was you.]
JIMMY: I don't—
EL GALLITO: *¿El cadaver? No mames, era tuyo güey.* [The corpse? Was you.]

> JIMMY *goes to hit* EL GALLITO *but* EL GALLITO *grabs his hand and forces it down.*

> EL GALLITO *forces his cigarette to* JIMMY*'s flesh.* EL GALLITO *counts.*

Uno, dos, tres, cuatro, cinco, seis, siete, ocho, nueve, nueve, nueve, nueve diez.

> EL GALLITO *withdraws the cigarette.*

Muy bien. [Very good.]

> EL GALLITO *kisses the burn.*

And we are in:

KINGS CROSS UNDER THE COCA-COLA SIGN

Heavy traffic.

JIMMY*'s phone rings.*

JIMMY: Yeah what? In the Cross. Why? Fuck. When? Yeah. Yeah I'll be there.

> JIMMY *ends the call. He takes a moment to think.*

Fuck. Fuck.

> JIMMY *grins.*

> JIMMY *hails a cab.*

> DARRYN SHINE *enters, wearing thongs and a hospital gown and carrying a plastic bag of clothing.*

DARRYN: Jimmy? Jimmy?

Jimmy, it's Darryn. Darryn fucking Shine. Luke's brother. You know, Luke's big bro?

> JIMMY *stares blankly at* DARRYN.

You remember Luke?

JIMMY: Yeah.

DARRYN: Can't forget Luke. Can't forget Lukey.

What are you doing in the Cross, man?

JIMMY: Leaving.

DARRYN: Where you going?

JIMMY: None of your business.

DARRYN: You're not goin' to Vietnamatta are ya?

JIMMY: No.

DARRYN: What about Penrif can I get a ride to Penrif?

JIMMY: No.

DARRYN: How will I get home?

JIMMY: Catch a fucking bus.

> DARRYN *stands next to* JIMMY *and waits.*

DARRYN: There's a cab. He's got his lights on.

> DARRYN *hails the cab.*

Lick my sperm mother-fucker! What's his problem? There's another one. Crawl back inside your mum's vagina! Fuck you yeah fuck you come here and say it.

JIMMY: Darren.

DARRYN: Yeah Jimmy?

JIMMY: Step away.

DARRYN: Why?

JIMMY: You're in my fucking face.

> DARRYN *takes a small step back.*

ACT THREE 71

Further.

    DARRYN *takes another small step back.*

Further.

DARRYN: It's the gown. It's the hospital gown isn't it? I just discharged meself from St Vinnie's. Been in iso for three days. Guess what Jimmy?

JIMMY: —

DARRYN: I'm not wearing any undies.

JIMMY: I can see that Darryn.

DARRYN: The psych nurses nick your jocks while you're off your chops. They reckon you'll hang yourself with 'em but they never give 'em back. They sell 'em to the other patients on the black. Hey you got something going haven't you Jimmy?

JIMMY: What?

DARRYN: Come on share the love.

JIMMY: Why are you asking me that?

DARRYN: I'm just putting the feelers out.

JIMMY: Who told you that?

DARRYN: No-one.

JIMMY: Who the fuck have you been talking to?

DARRYN: No-one I swear Jimmy I swear I'm just putting the feelers out. 'Cause I'm happy to do a trip. Asia. India. Love Asian food, love Thai, love curry. Wherever. Whenever. I'm flexible. Spread the word will you Jimmy? I'm not shoving it up me bum. Draw the line there. Yeah. That shit splits in your rectum mid-air it's sayonara. Good way to go but no, it's not going up me bum for all the ice in China. Hey can you say, 'Ni hao', Jimmy? Ice is taking off in China. We could be drug lords over there, Jimmy. *Ni hao*, that's all you need to know. We could set up a meth lab in a mountain village. Seriously seriously you and me Jimmy your brains my brawns. Are you in or are you in?

    JIMMY *ignores* DARRYN.

    Silence.

Hey I'm getting on the rock you wanna score some rock with me Jimmy?

JIMMY: I would rather neck myself.

    Pause.

DARRYN: Fair enough.
> I heard you was clean. Respect.
>> DARRYN *checks out* JIMMY*'s clothes.*
>> Nice threads. [*Pause.*] Can you lend me fifty bucks?

JIMMY: Fifty? That all Darryn? Sure you don't want any more?

DARRYN: Yeah no actually actually better make it eighty pay you back Thursdy.
>> JIMMY *looks through his wallet.*

JIMMY: Let me just see / what I've…

DARRYN: We can go to the A.T.M. there's an A.T.M. round the corner / which bank are you—?

JIMMY: Here we go.
>> JIMMY *tips his small change onto the street.*

DARRYN: I'm Lukey's brother.

JIMMY: I know.

DARRYN: Luke Shine. He deserved that name. He was born to shine. Like that song. Until you come along rubbed his face in shit. Got him on the rock.

JIMMY: He was a big boy.

DARRYN: You'd know. Good to see you're clean now Jimmy. He's dead you're clean.
>> DARRYN *eyes the coins on the ground.*

JIMMY: Quick.
> Before someone else gets it.
>> JIMMY *makes chicken sounds as* DARRYN *gets down on his hands and knees and picks up the coins.*
>
> Missed one.
>> DARRYN *reaches for it.*
>> JIMMY *stands on the coin.*
>
> Sorry man here it is.
>> JIMMY *takes his foot off the coin.*
>> DARRYN *reaches for it again.* JIMMY *stands on it.*

JIMMY *takes his foot off the coin.*

Go on.
Take it.
It's yours.
Take it.

    DARRYN *picks up the last coin, pockets it.* JIMMY *hails a cab.*

DARRYN: You're dead.
JIMMY: What was that?

    JIMMY *stops, turns around.*

DARRYN: Every cunt in the Cross knows you done a pork roll. You're a dead man.

    JIMMY *launches a viscous drop kick at* DARRYN*'s face.*

    JIMMY *notices a spot of blood on his calf-skin loafers. He bends down to wipe it off.*

    When he looks up he sees ALVARO.

    ALVARO *is carrying a rooster in a hessian bag.*

    And we are:

AT THE PELEA DE GALLOS, OUTSKIRTS OF COROICO

JIMMY *is drinking Coca-Cola.*

JIMMY: Hello again.
Photo?

    ALVARO *cautiously approaches* JIMMY.

    JIMMY *takes a picture with his phone.*

    JIMMY *shows* ALVARO *the image.*

    ALVARO *stares at the image, he doesn't recognise himself.*

That's you.

    ALVARO *tries to take the phone from* JIMMY.

No no no I need that.
Coke… Coca-Cola?

JIMMY *gives his Coke to* ALVARO.

ALVARO *sculls it.*

It's Alvaro isn't it?

ALVARO *is silent.*

Mi nombre es Jimmy. [My name is Jimmy.]
Did I say that right?

ALVARO *doesn't respond.*

What's in the bag?

JIMMY *looks inside the bag.*

Is that Pablo?

ALVARO *nods.*

As in Escobar?

ALVARO *nods.*

Then I am betting two hundred pesos on Pablo. [*Pause.*] You know a rooster woke me at four a.m. this morning?
Was it him?

JIMMY *crows and then mimes strangling a rooster's neck.*

ALVARO *retreats.*

GRUBBE: Monte's out on bail.

JIMMY *swings around to see* GRUBBE.

JIMMY: That was a joke. It was a—
I wouldn't do that.

And we are in:

A BAR, REDFERN

JIMMY: He can't be.
GRUBBE: Fifty grand says he can.
JIMMY: No.
GRUBBE: I've spent this beautiful Sydney sunny day in an interview room cooped up with the cocky prick.
We followed your tip-off, searched the house in Woollahra.

ACT THREE

JIMMY: I told you not to do that.
GRUBBE: Child and pregnant wife were present.
That was pleasant.
JIMMY: He doesn't keep it there, why would he keep it there? I told you that.
GRUBBE: The boy's a trip.
JIMMY: What? Why?
GRUBBE: His drawings. The cocks. We had a nice little chat.
JIMMY: There's nothing there.
GRUBBE: Yeah we discovered that.
JIMMY: You don't think to give me some warning?
GRUBBE: We like to keep a few things up our sleeve Jimmy.
JIMMY: Fuck you very much.
GRUBBE: So while we raked the home with a fine-tooth comb we searched the St Leonard's storage unit.
What did we find?
JIMMY: His supply yeah?
GRUBBE: Perhaps you're referring to his impressive collection of French reds?
JIMMY: He's got at least twenty keys of coke. I put it there myself.
GRUBBE: Yeah?
JIMMY: Yeah.
GRUBBE: Fucking where?

Beat.

JIMMY: He's moved it. He must have moved it.
GRUBBE: He's cool as a cucumber too, didn't even break a sweat over the crime scene pics of his old mate Christos. Say goodbye to your four and a half star.
JIMMY: Hey?
GRUBBE: You'll be lucky if you say g'day to Sunday.
JIMMY: I've signed a memorandum of understanding. I'll go to the fucking ombudsman.
GRUBBE: You'll go to the ombudsman will you? Do you even know what an ombudsman is, Jimmy?
JIMMY: I know I've rights under the witness protection act.
GRUBBE: But you didn't deliver your side of the contract.

JIMMY: I fucking did.
GRUBBE: Well let's see it.
JIMMY: What?
GRUBBE: The Memorandum of Understandings. The M.O.U. sets out very clearly everything on offer so let's have a look.
JIMMY: I don't have it.
GRUBBE: Why not?
JIMMY: You have it.
GRUBBE: I don't have it Jimmy.
JIMMY: You said that me having a copy was a security risk.
GRUBBE: If you don't have a copy…
JIMMY: You said that's how it works: the A.C.C. keeps both copies.
GRUBBE: Can't recall saying that. Now if you don't have it—
JIMMY: You have it.
GRUBBE: —how do you know the M.O.U. exists? How do you know you didn't just dream it?

Beat.

JIMMY: I signed it.
GRUBBE: Sure about that?
JIMMY: I signed it in front of two witnesses.
GRUBBE: Known to you?
JIMMY: Known to you.
GRUBBE: Names?

Beat.

JIMMY: You cunt.
GRUBBE: Their names Jimmy can you remember the names of the witnesses?
JIMMY: You can't fucking do this.
EL GALLITO: *Apunta tu fierro.* [Draw your gun.]

    EL GALLITO *appears at the bar.* JIMMY *swings around.*

JIMMY: It's out. It's all over Kings Cross that I've rolled.
GRUBBE: Whoopsy.
EL GALLITO: *Apunta tu fierro, culero.* [Draw your gun, faggot.]
JIMMY: Does Monte know?
GRUBBE: —

    JIMMY *draws the gun from inside his sleeve.*

ACT THREE

JIMMY: Does he know?
GRUBBE: That's a toy Jimmy.
JIMMY: No. No it's—
GRUBBE: I'm afraid so Jimmy that is not a real gun.
EL GALLITO: *Dispara.* [Pull the trigger.]
GRUBBE: Is this a game Jimmy?

    GRUBBE *moves towards* JIMMY.

JIMMY: Don't fucking…
GRUBBE: A game that little boys play?

    You want to play with me?

EL GALLITO: *Metele una bala en el cuello cabrón.* [Shoot the motherfucker in the neck.]

    GRUBBE *swipes the gun from* JIMMY *and slaps him.*

JIMMY: I'm dead. I'm a dead man.
EL GALLITO: *Ya te huelo, güey.* [Yes, I can already smell you.]

    JIMMY *turns to* EL GALLITO.

JIMMY: Shut up.

    EL GALLITO *laughs at* JIMMY.

    Shut the fuck up.

GRUBBE: Look, I can see you're stressed. It's very common for people in the program to experience emotional duress, jumping at shadows, looking over their shoulder to see who's behind them.

    With the cooperation you've shown so far I'm pretty sure I can get you, your sister and your nephew onto the top of the public housing list. You can probably move in in time for Christmas. Imagine that, Jimmy. Your very own inner-city high-rise in Surry Hills. I hear some apartments even have a view of the harbour. That'll be a step up from Penrith.

    EL GALLITO *whispers to* JIMMY.

EL GALLITO: *Está muerta.* [She's dead.]
JIMMY: She's dead.
GRUBBE: Who's dead Jimmy?
JIMMY: The girl with the pony. Your daughter. She's dead, isn't she?
EL GALLITO: *Es un esqueleto.* [She's a skeleton.]

GRUBBE: Who told you that?
JIMMY: She was a junkie.
GRUBBE: I'd shut your mouth.
JIMMY: A worthless fucking junkie.
GRUBBE: Isn't that the pot calling the kettle black?
JIMMY: That's why you want La Madre.
GRUBBE: Is it?
JIMMY: She fucked your daughter over didn't she?
GRUBBE: You're full of insight aren't you?
JIMMY: You'll never get La Madre.
GRUBBE: Won't I just?
JIMMY: She'll die before you get to her.
GRUBBE: Keep digging.
EL GALLITO: *Embrujará tus sueoñs.* [She'll haunt your dreams.]
JIMMY: She'll fuck you from her grave.

> GRUBBE *punches* JIMMY, *he falls.* JIMMY *tries to get up.*

EL GALLITO: *Levantate.* [Get up.]
GRUBBE: Stay down.

> EL GALLITO *lifts* JIMMY *by the hair.*

EL GALLITO: *Levantate.* [Get up.]
GRUBBE: Stay down.

> EL GALLITO *thrusts* JIMMY *towards* GRUBBE, *forcing him to fight.*

EL GALLITO: *Pelea.* [Fight.]
GRUBBE: You're a glutton for punishment.

> EL GALLITO *circles* GRUBBE *and* JIMMY *as they fight, goading* JIMMY.

> EL GALLITO *is full of rage.*

EL GALLITO: *¿Lo estas chingando o peleando?* [Are you fucking him or fighting him?]
Arrancale la piel. [Rip his flesh.]
Sacale los hojos. [Claw his eyes.]
Rompele la cara. [Break his face.]
Comele el Corazón. [Eat his heart.]

> GRUBBE *holds* JIMMY *down.*

ACT THREE

As GRUBBE *speaks, his accent slips into German. He is* BARBIE.

GRUBBE: Listen to me *du verdammter arschficker*. La Madre had better get her fucking gravestone ready. I will gut her like a *pollito* [chicken], just like I did her *scheisskopf* [shithead] son.

    JIMMY *recognises* BARBIE *in* GRUBBE*'s voice.*

JIMMY: Who the fuck—?
GRUBBE: *Öffne deine Augen.* [Open your eyes.]

    GRUBBE*'s voice returns.*

Now you go back to Monte and you do whatever you have to do to get me the evidence I need to make that blue-blood fucker squeal.
Then and only then can we talk again about your M.O. fucking U.
Do you hear me you fucking junkie?

    GRUBBE *is gone.*

    EL GALLITO *unzips his fly and pisses on* JIMMY.

END OF ACT THREE

ACT FOUR

JIMMY *is alone. He leans down to pick up the toy gun. He looks closely at it.*

JIMMY *slips the gun up his sleeve.*

SCARLET *and* ALVARO *appear.*

And we are in:

A PLAYGROUND, CABRAMATTA

JIMMY: Where's Monte?
SCARLET: Oli go and play hey.

    ALVARO *leaves.*

JIMMY: Something's wrong with him.
SCARLET: He's sick.
JIMMY: No that's not—Where's Monte?
SCARLET: Jimmy—
JIMMY: Told Monte to meet me here.
SCARLET: Jimmy—
JIMMY: I'm calling him.
SCARLET: We're being watched.

    JIMMY *ends the call.* JIMMY *looks around.*

Remember this used to be where all the junkies scored? Do you remember that feral sandpit? You'd have to pick out all the needles before you could play in it. Every week someone'd O.D. in the toilet block. What a shit place to grow up.
It's nice now.
It's clean.
They didn't find anything, a few grams that's all. He'll be doing community service for a year.
JIMMY: Lucky.
SCARLET: Not luck. It's foresight.
JIMMY: Monte moved the gear.

ACT FOUR

SCARLET: —
JIMMY: I didn't think / you—
SCARLET: You think I'm blind Jimmy?
> Open your eyes. I've earned this. I deserve it.
> We need to clean this up—
>   *Pause.*

JIMMY: Where is it?
SCARLET: Remember when Mum was sick? No probably not fuck knows where you were somewhere out of it.
> I took care of her, nursed her for two years.
> One day when I popped out to the shops get some smokes someone broke in.
> They smashed the back laundry window with a brick, went straight to Mum's room, stole her meds, all her morphine. Knew what they were looking for.
> What a cunt, huh?
> What a cunt act.
>>   JIMMY *knows she knows.*
> You owe this family Jimmy.
> Don't you think?
>>   JIMMY *nods.*
> Feel like a trip to Double Bay?

JIMMY: What's in Double Bay?
>   SCARLET *gives* JIMMY *a set of keys.*

SCARLET: An apartment.
JIMMY: Who's?
SCARLET: Yours.
>   *Beat.*

JIMMY: Say again.
SCARLET: We bought it the same time we purchased your place in Penrith.
JIMMY: Why don't I know this?
SCARLET: Congratulations Jimmy. Welcome to the East Side.
> Second bedroom in the built-ins. The boxes are there. Plus cash.
> Drive out to Blacktown, go to the train station, carpark city side.

At 3.45 p.m. you'll meet a man called Hung in a silver Nissan sedan. Give him the cash, don't say anything.

JIMMY: What do I do with the gear?

SCARLET: Go to Woolworths buy some gladbags and bury it in the bush. Any questions, Jimmy?

JIMMY: Shit hits the fan I'm the pawn. Is that the idea?

SCARLET: —

JIMMY: Is that the idea?

> SCARLET *touches* JIMMY *on the face. She gives* JIMMY *the keys to the Double Bay apartment.*

SCARLET: It's time to grow up.

We don't want to lose you.

> ALVARO *enters carrying a blood-stained hessian bag.*

Oli, say goodbye to Uncle Jimmy.

JIMMY: What's in the bag?

> ALVARO *is silent.*

SCARLET: We have to go.

JIMMY: Wait. [*To* ALVARO] What's in the bag?

> ALVARO *is silent.*

Show me.

> JIMMY *draws his gun. It's real.*

Quietos.

SCARLET: Jimmy.

JIMMY: It's okay.

SCARLET: Jimmy is that—?

JIMMY: It's okay—

SCARLET: Jimmy.

JIMMY: —it's just a game we play.

Isn't it?

ALVARO: I have to die now.

> JIMMY *lowers the gun.*

> SCARLET *is gone.*

> JIMMY *is alone, he looks at the keys to the Double Bay apartment.*

JIMMY: Fuck you, Monte.

ACT FOUR

THE PELEA DE GALLOS, OUTSKIRTS OF COROICO

BARBIE *enters with a rooster cage.*

BARBIE: All over Latin America everyone has heard of Barbie's champion birds.

>BARBIE *holds the cage up to* JIMMY.

>Now, when you look into the eyes of Señor Gallo what do you see?

>JIMMY *looks inside the cage.*

JIMMY: Fear?

BARBIE: Fear. *Ja.* Rage. Yes. These creatures are born for violence. It is why God made them, to kill each other. It is their nature.
The *pelea de gallos* is the theatre of life. Hatred, cruelty, violence, death. Our lives reduced to a drama.

>ALVARO *appears with a rooster in a hessian bag.*

>BARBIE *calls* ALVARO *over.*

>Boy, come here.

>ALVARO *approaches* BARBIE.

JIMMY: How old is he?

BARBIE: *Siete… ocho…*

JIMMY: Same age as my nephew.

BARBIE: A little cock but a good worker, aren't you, Alvaro?

>BARBIE *strokes the boy's head.*

>You want him?

JIMMY: What?

BARBIE: You know for the night?

>MONTE *arrives.*

JIMMY: / No. No.

BARBIE: Ah, and here is your partner.
So we begin.

>BARBIE *and* ALVARO *withdraw a handful of feathers from the bag.*

>*Slowly they begin to circle the pit.*

>*The feathers are thrown into the air in a violent clash of colour.*

A dance of death.

BARBIE and ALVARO's hands are covered in blood.

ALVARO's rooster is dead.

ALVARO picks up each feather and places it in the hessian bag.

BARBIE wipes his bloodied hands on his apron. He appears like The Butcher from the folktale.

Too bad, Alvaro. Pablo was no match for my champion. Next time, eh?

I will give you another cock to raise, okay?

MONTE: What happens now?

BARBIE: The winner consumes the loser.

JIMMY watches as ALVARO takes a small knife from his pocket.

MONTE: You're going to eat Pablo?

BARBIE: Of course.

Do you know what the locals call me? They call me El Carnicero. You know this word?

JIMMY: The Butcher.

BARBIE: *Muy bien.* [Very good.]

Do you know why they call me El Carnicero?

JIMMY: No.

BARBIE: Well, I love meat, *wurst*. I am German, *ja*.

ALVARO flies at BARBIE.

JIMMY intercepts, grabbing him. ALVARO drops the knife.

It's okay.

Let him go. It's okay.

Please.

JIMMY releases ALVARO.

BARBIE smiles.

Venga. [Come here.]

ALVARO approaches BARBIE.

It's okay.

It's okay.

ACT FOUR

Señor Barbie te quiere como un padre. [Señor Barbie loves you like a father.]
It's okay. It's okay.
    ALVARO *whispers in* BARBIE *ear.*
Ja.
Wait for me in the kitchen.
    ALVARO *runs off.*
    BARBIE *cleans Alvaro's knife.*
Do you know what he said to me just now?
Señor, no se olvide que soy delicado. [Señor, don't forget that I am soft.]
Don't forget that I am soft.
    Pause.
So, Monte.
MONTE: Yes?
BARBIE: Perhaps you are wondering why it is I ask you to come all this way down El Camino de la Muerte? The Road of Death?
    MONTE *nods.*
I ask you here because I must be sure that you young cocks have the stomach for the business.
MONTE: What's the verdict?
BARBIE: In Sydney you partner with La Madre, *ja*?
MONTE: That's right but she's—
BARBIE: And now you want to do business with El Carnicero?
MONTE: Why we're here.
BARBIE: No more La Madre, okay?
MONTE: It's an insatiable market we / could—
BARBIE: No more La Madre.
    Pause.
MONTE: Okay.
BARBIE: No problem?
MONTE: No problem.
BARBIE: [*to* JIMMY] Is there something troubling you my friend?

JIMMY *stares at* BARBIE.

MONTE: Jimmy?

Pause.

JIMMY: —

BARBIE: It's okay, don't worry.

Alvaro is going to take a little aeroplane ride.

And you, my friend, are going to help him pack.

BARBIE *produces a bottle of schnaps and glasses. He raises a toast.*

A toast to our new partnership.

Prost!

MONTE: *Prost!*

JIMMY *raises his glass.*

JIMMY: *Prost.*

JIMMY *swallows the shot.*

The scene morphs. BARBIE *and* MONTE *watch as* JIMMY *'feeds'* ALVARO *several small white balls.*

First, JIMMY *dips the ball in Coca-Cola.* ALVARO *opens his mouth.* BARBIE *counts.*

BARBIE: *Cuatro.*

JIMMY *feeds another ball to* ALVARO. *He swallows.*

Cinco.

And another.

Seis.

JIMMY *watches* BARBIE *remove his butcher's apron and morph into* GRUBBE.

GRUBBE *interrogates* MONTE.

GRUBBE: Monte, did you know the Mexican wave was first invented in Monterrey, Mexico, during a football matched between Tigres and Monterrey? During the half-time the players were taking longer than expected to return to the field. The crowd grew anxious and the organisers were trying to entertain them by throwing balls as presents.

ACT FOUR

And that's how they created *'la ola'*, which after a few goes made its way round the stadium.

Now, after the five kilos we found in the boot of your Merc, I think you're feeling just a little bit anxious, Monte. Just like that crowd in Monterrey, so why don't we try the Mexican wave? Let's try it together.

Okay and here we go.

    GRUBBE *stands up, raising his arms.*

And here we go… Monte, your turn. And here we go… and… here we go… I can't do the Mexican wave on my own, Monte. And here we go…

    MONTE *stands.*

    He sits.

    He stands.

    He sits.

    He stands.

    As he sits EL GALLITO *stuffs his mouth with feathers.*

    Darkness.

    And we are:

IN JIMMY'S APARTMENT, PENRITH

EL GALLITO*'s voice is heard.*

As the scene progresses, the light increases.

EL GALLITO *is dressing in a funeral suit.*

EL GALLITO: Last night, while you are sleeping, I enter your head. You dream you are on a bus. You are travelling down El Camino de la Muerte. It is dark on the road, pissing rain. *Estas cagado de miedo.* Your knuckles white from gripping the front seat as the bus takes the narrow turns. In the seat in front of you, a very old *Señora* is praying. Her hands like bones fingering the rosario. The bus turns the bend and there is a truck coming the other way. There is no room for both vehicles to pass so the drivers draw straws to decide who will reverse. *Mala suerte*, the driver of your bus draws short. So slowly the bus reverses down El Camino de la Muerte. And then, the tyre slips, the road gives way and the wheels of the bus start to tip over the edge of the cliff. The *Señora* turns to you… her face has no flesh. *Un esqueleto. Dientes* are broken. Her *heuses* bleached white. The sockets of her *hojos* are empty. She smiles at you. At you and no-one else. And then the metal groans and twists and the bus slips over the edge of the cliff. *Te caes.* And as the bus crashes into the hungry *boca* of the *jungla*, you feel your spine snap. You feel your *corazón* stop. You feel your blood drain. Your *huesos* grow *frios*. Then it is dark. Then it is quiet. And then—

JIMMY *wakes in semi-darkness, gasping for air.*

¿Cómo sabes que esto no es un sueño? [How do you know this is not the dream?]

How do you know this is not the nightmare?

JIMMY *smells the air.*

JIMMY: That smell?
EL GALLITO: *El olor de la muerte.* [The smell of death.]

EL GALLITO *collects a bunch of* cempasûchil *(marigold) flowers.*

EL GALLITO *breaks one off and places it in his lapel.*

JIMMY: Where are you going?
EL GALLITO: *Mi madre esté muerta.* [My mother is dead.]
JIMMY: Your mother? She's dead?

Lo lamento. [I'm sorry.]

EL GALLITO *ignores him.*

When will you be back?
EL GALLITO: I won't.
JIMMY: You're leaving?
EL GALLITO: *Adios.* [Goodbye.]
JIMMY: *Te amo.* [I love you.]

EL GALLITO *ignores him.*

Do you love me?

EL GALLITO *whispers in* JIMMY*'s ear.*

ACT FOUR

EL GALLITO: *Te* [I]
    Odio [hate]
    a [your]
    muerte. [guts.]
JIMMY: How can you—?
EL GALLITO: *Mi pecho es un hueco.* [My chest is empty.]
    Mi estomago un vacio. [My stomach a cavity.]
JIMMY: Stay.
EL GALLITO: *Pinche cabrón.* [You're weak as piss.]
JIMMY: Fuck you.
EL GALLITO: *No tienes ni verga.* [You have no cock.]
JIMMY: Fuck you.
EL GALLITO: *No tienes ni madre.* [You have no mother.]
JIMMY: Fuck you.

    EL GALLITO *goes to leave.*

You're not going.
EL GALLITO: *Entonces luchame.* [Fight me.]

    EL GALLITO *slaps* JIMMY.

Cortame. [Cut me.]

    He slaps him again.

Matame. [Kill me.]

    And again.

Consumime o me voy para siempre. [Eat me or I'm gone from you forever.]

    EL GALLITO *has* JIMMY *by the neck.*

Tu o yo. [You or I.]

    EL GALLITO *throws* JIMMY *to the floor.*

Elige. [Choose.]

    JIMMY *cowers.*

Entonces, sufre. [Then suffer.]

    EL GALLITO *walks away.*

JIMMY: *Me cago en tu madre muerta.* [I shit on your dead mother.]

EL GALLITO stops.

Did you hear me?

JIMMY runs at EL GALLITO

EL GALLITO *draws a box cutter and turns, cutting* JIMMY*'s hand.*

JIMMY *nurses his hand,* EL GALLITO *sneers at him.*

EL GALLITO *drops the box cutter and turns to leave.*

JIMMY *lunges at* EL GALLITO *again, slicing him across the abdomen.*

EL GALLITO *pulls* JIMMY *to him and whispers.*

EL GALLITO: Don't forget that I am soft.

They fall together. EL GALLITO *is dead.*

JIMMY *opens a can of Coca-Cola, drinks it.*

He then callously strips EL GALLITO *of his bloodied suit.*

JIMMY *dresses in* EL GALLITO*'s clothes.*

He picks up each marigold flower and makes a new bouquet.

And we are:

AT LA MADRE'S FUNERAL IN PUNCHBOWL

JIMMY *listens as* GRUBBE *finishes the story.*

GRUBBE: Once upon a time in Punchbowl there lived an old woman known to many as La Madre. The Mother. She lived alone and simply, as if she were a poor woman with barely enough *tortilla* for her table. In truth, she owned more than you could ever imagine. But La Madre had no desire for wealth, she hungered only for revenge. Years passed and La Madre's craving grew and grew and grew until one day La Madre went to The Physician to complain of stomach ache.

The Physician took La Madre's blood and tested it. When he saw the results he shook his head. He had bad news for La Madre. She had cancer and only three months to live.

On the night of La Madre's death, she wept and wept and wept and before long her tears of rage filled a large cooking pot. In this cooking pot of tears La Madre made *mole negro*.

ACT FOUR

To the pot, La Madre added cinnamon, garlic, banana, onion, fat, raisins, thyme and the most powerful ingredient of all, Coca-Cola.

When the *mole* was rich and ready La Madre filled a bowl with the black sauce and she opened an ice-cold can of Coca-Cola which was her son's favourite.

Then La Madre closed her eyes and died.

>JIMMY *leaves the marigold flowers and is gone.*
>
>GRUBBE *remains.*

THE END

Belvoir and State Theatre Company of South Australia present

Mortido

By **ANGELA BETZIEN**
Director **LETICIA CÁCERES**

This production of Mortido *opened at the Dunstan Playhouse on 20 October 2015 and Belvoir St Theatre on Wednesday 11 November 2015.*

Set & Costume Designer **ROBERT COUSINS**
Lighting Designer **GEOFF COBHAM**
Composer **THE SWEATS**
Sound Designer **NATE EDMONDSON**
Dramaturg **ANTHEA WILLIAMS**
Movement Director **SCOTT WITT**
Assistant Director **RACHEL CHANT**
Dialect Coach **JENNIFER WHITE**
Stage Manager **LUKE McGETTIGAN**
Assistant Stage Manager **SEAN PROUDE**

With
Oliver / Alvaro* **TOBY CHALLENOR**
Jimmy **TOM CONROY**
Oliver / Alvaro* **OTIS JAI DHANJI**
Oliver / Alvaro** **CALIN DIAMOND**
Detective Grubbe / others **COLIN FRIELS**
Oliver / Alvaro** **MATT GOLDWYN**
Scarlet / Sybille **LOUISA MIGNONE**
Monte / Darren Shine **RENATO MUSOLINO**
El Gallito **DAVID VALENCIA**

* Sydney season
** Adelaide season

Mortido is a co-commission with Playwriting Australia

playwriting
australia

PRODUCTION THANKS Whitney Richards (chaperone); Sophie Fletcher; Rock Surfers Theatre Company.
PHOTOGRAPHY Brett Boardman
DESIGN Alphabet Studio

Writer's Note
Angela Betzien

I began thinking about this play in late 2011 during rehearsals for *The Dark Room* for Belvoir. Around this time, journalist Joel Meares wrote 'Score, Chop, Snort: Sydney's Cocaine Blizzard'[1], an investigation into the consumption of cocaine in the Emerald City. At the time, most of Sydney's *snow, parrot, pearl, charlie, flake, blow, base, zip*, whatever you choose to call it, came direct from Mexico, where in the last decade a bloody drug war has resulted in more than 60,000 deaths.

Cocaine is a drug of image, individualism, ego, sex, greed, lies and short-term gain. It's a drug that encapsulates the values of the here and now, of a first world afflicted with 'affluenza' – symptoms of which include excessive consumption, aspiration and blindness to the plight of the disadvantaged.

Mortido is part of a cycle of crime dramas I have written over the last decade. Most of these plays have been developed with director Leticia Cáceres and our independent company RealTV. Our fascination with crime connects with our desire to make political theatre, to tell stories of money, power and injustice. Like many of my peers, I've also been inspired by the 'Golden Age' of television and the emergence of popular crime dramas that have transcended our expectations of the genre.

Playwright Simon Stephens said, 'I have this intuitive and completely unresearched notion that crime fiction is the narrative form that has defined the last ten years, in the way that the western defined the '50s. I wonder if we are operating in a culture with a sense that something awful has been done, and we want to find who did it.'[2]

What if that 'something awful' is global capitalism? What if it's the cruel and destructive pursuit of profit over people?

In the 1920s, after the unprecedented atrocities of World War One, Freud began to develop the theory of the death drive, the instinct of all living things to return to an inanimate state. This theory was further developed by his contemporaries and was often referred to as 'thanatos' or 'mortido' and was used by some to explain the destructiveness in individuals, groups and nations.

I wonder, is the destructive drive of mortido in all of us? Is it symbiotically linked with our drive for life, for self-preservation? In a certain set of circumstances, in a certain climate, does one rise up to master the other?

Writing *Mortido* has been a thrilling adventure and I'm proud to say I've travelled to every location in the story: from the barrios of Mexico, to the hipster hub of Kreuzberg, from La Paz down El Camino de la Muerte to Coroico, and from a CBD nightclub to the pho-infused backstreets of Cabramatta.

I'd like to thank everyone for joining me on this wild ride.

I'd particularly like to thank Belvoir and Playwriting Australia for commissioning this work, and Leticia Cáceres for her perseverance, passion and politics.

---

1 Meares, Joel, 'Score, Chop, Snort: Sydney's Cocaine Blizzard', *the (sydney) magazine*, reproduced in the *Newcastle Herald* online, 26 October 2011.

2 'Interview: Simon Stephens talks on his new play *Three Kingdoms*', *Evening Standard* online, 3 May 2012.

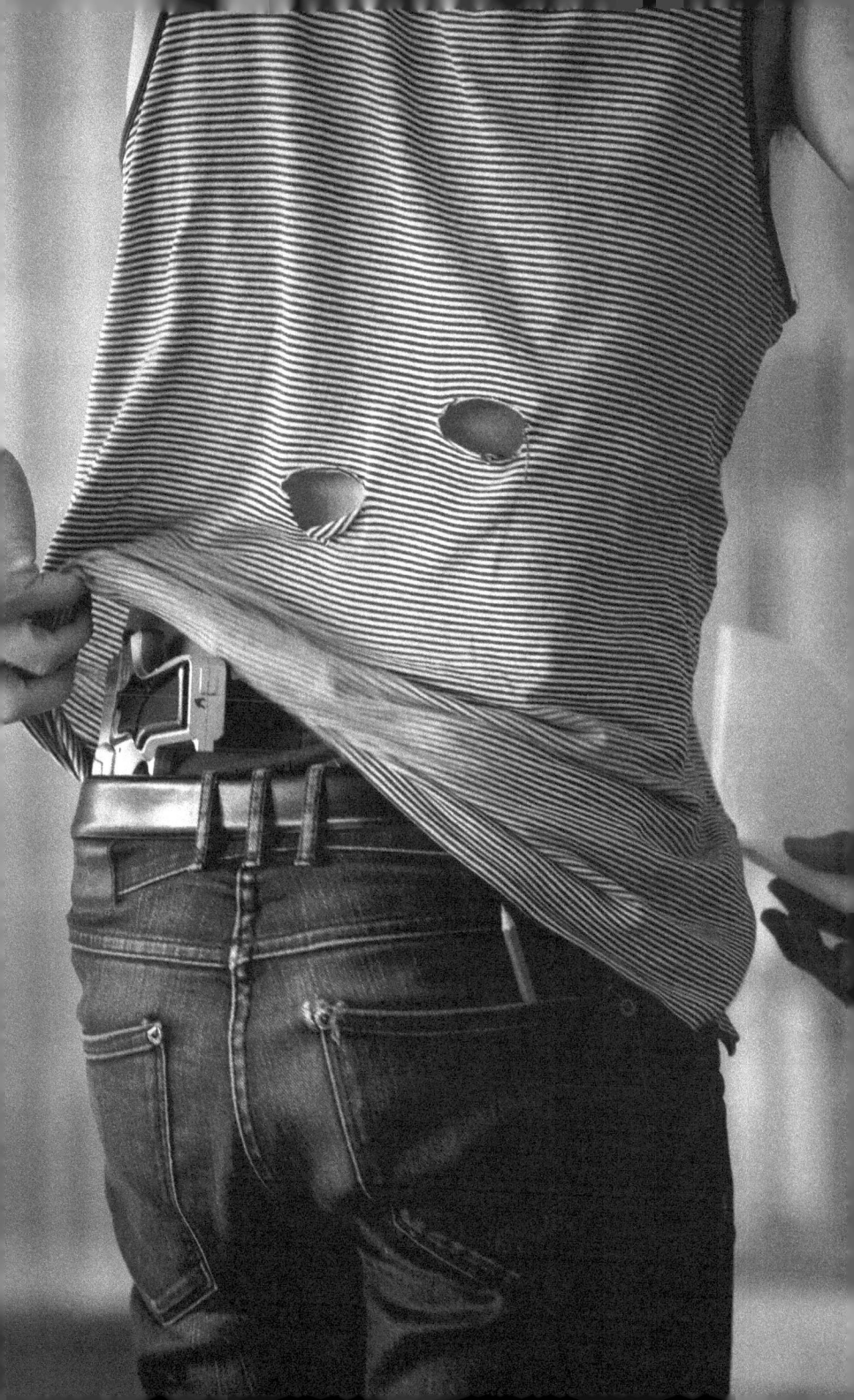

Director's Note
Leticia Cáceres

We live in a world of excess: excess information, food, porn, news, drugs, advertisements, social media. Everything we consume is sanitised and neatly packaged. We can happily leave our brains out of the transaction because all the thinking and feeling has been done for us, no imagination required.

Our current saturated cultural climate makes us superbly adept at absorbing and processing information, but we are currently at risk of experiencing a kind of atrophy of the imagination. So what? you might ask. Why do you care so much about our imagination? It is through our imagination that we might envisage a fairer world.

So how do you do that as a theatre-maker? For me, making *Mortido* has been a process of distillation, of creating space for audiences to exercise their own imaginations. Every step of the way we've asked ourselves: what elements do we really need to tell this tale? To what extent can we trust the audience to listen, to feel, to know, to put the pieces of the puzzle together?

I hope *Mortido* is more than a nice night out at the theatre. I hope it is a workout for the brain (and hopefully the heart!). I hope it is an invitation to imagine the unimaginable.

I want to thank Belvoir and State Theatre Company of South Australia for their faith in *Mortido*. I want to thank the cast and creatives for their ferocious determination to tell this story. And I want to thank Angela Betzien for her unwavering belief in the subversive power of theatre.

Leticia Cáceres

Biographies

ANGELA BETZIEN Writer

Angela is a multi-award-winning writer and a founding member of independent theatre company Real TV; her work has toured widely across Australia and internationally and has been published in multiple languages. Belvoir's production of her play *The Dark Room* won the 2011 Sydney Theatre Award for Best New Australian Work and had a reading at London's National Theatre in 2015 as part of her studio attachment there. In 2014 Angela was awarded the Patrick White Fellowship at Sydney Theatre Company. Her other work includes *War Crimes*, which won the Kit Denton Disfellowship and QLD Literary Award; *Children of the Black Skirt*, which toured Australian schools for three years and won the 2005 Drama Victoria Award for Best Performance by a Theatre Company for Secondary Schools; and *Hoods*, which toured extensively throughout Australia and internationally to Cortile Theatre Im Hof, Italy, and Dschungel Wien Theaterhaus, Austria in 2010. Angela's other work includes *Where in the World is Frank Sparrow?* (commissioned by Graffiti Theatre, Ireland); *The Girl Who Cried Wolf* (commissioned by Sydney Opera House:Ed); *Helicopter* (Melbourne Theatre Company); *Tall Man* (Creative Regions); *The Teenage Alchemist* (commissioned by ATYP and Camp Quality); *Princess of Suburbia* (Real TV); and *The Kingswood Kids* (La Boite). The European premiere of *Helicopter* will be presented by the National Theatre of Norway in late 2015. Angela is also the recipient of a 2015 Kim Williams Playwriting Fellowship.

LETICIA CÁCERES Director

Leticia is currently Associate Director of Melbourne Theatre Company. Her credits include *Miss Julie*, *The Dark Room* (nominated for seven Sydney Theatre Awards) (Belvoir); *Birdland*, *The Effect* (nominated for three Green Room Awards), *Yellow Moon* (winner of a Drama Victoria Award and nominated for four Green Room Awards), *Cock*, *Constellations*, *Helicopter*, *Random* (nominated for three Green Room Awards) (Melbourne Theatre Company); *Death and the Maiden* (Melbourne Theatre Company/Sydney Theatre Company); *Memory of Water*, *Far Away*, *The Orphanage Project* (Queensland Theatre Company); *War Crimes, Hoods, Children of the Black Skirt* (Sydney Opera House, Melbourne Arts Centre, Brisbane Powerhouse). Leticia is the co-founder of nationally acclaimed RealTV, whose work has toured nationally and internationally. *Hoods* won the 2009 Matilda Award for Best Independent Production, the 2007 AWGIE Award for Theatre for Young Audiences and received a 2008 Helpmann nomination. Leticia's previous professional appointments include Intern Director and Associate Director for Queensland Theatre Company and Artistic Director of Tantrum Youth Theatre.

TOBY CHALLENOR Oliver / Alvaro (Sydney season)

Toby has been singing, dancing, performing and competing since the age of three. He first appeared on stage at Belvoir in *Nora* (2014). Apart from over a dozen TV commercials in the last few years, his television credits include *Underbelly Badness* as Blake Dokic, and a role in the Catalyst series on ABCTV. Toby's film credits include the short films *Way Out* and *The Immortal*, and the feature film *Felony* in which he plays Jake Toohey alongside Joel Edgerton and Melissa George. Apart from his love of the performing arts, Toby is a keen sportsman and excels at both cricket and rugby league. He comes from a true showbiz family, being one of four children all of whom are involved in the arts. Toby is very excited to be back at Belvoir.

RACHEL CHANT Assistant Director

Rachel is an Associate Director at Rock Surfers Theatre Company, founding director of independent theatre company Eclective Productions and Festival Director for Bondi Feast festival. She has a Masters of Applied Theatre Studies and a Bachelor of Arts (Theatre/Journalism) from the University of New England. Her directing credits include *Decay* (Old505 Theatre); *Blue Italian + Nil by Sea* (Site+Sound Festival); *When the Rain Stops Falling* (New Theatre); *Machine* (Old505 Theatre); *The Pitchfork Disney* (Sidetrack Theatre); *Hybrid Dream: a postdramatic reimagining of Strindberg's Dream Plays* (PACT Theatre); *24 Hour Party Playwright 2014/2015* (Rock Surfers Theatre Company); *Somewhere Over the Happy Rainbow* (Cut&Paste); and *Frenzy for Two* (UNE Arts Theatre). Rachel's assistant directing credits include *The Way Things Work* (Rock Surfers Theatre Company); *Sweet Nothings* (ATYP/pantsguys Productions); and *The Ham Funeral* (New Theatre). Rachel was a 2014 Playwriting Australia Dramaturgy intern and a member of Playwriting Australia's inaugural Directors' Studio.

GEOFF COBHAM Lighting Designer

Geoff has worked as a production manager, lighting designer, set designer, event producer and venue designer. His love of light and dance has led him to work with many of Australia's top choreographers and allowed him to explore the endless combinations of colour, angle, intensity and movement of light. He has also lit museums, buildings, public art and freeways. Geoff has produced many outdoor events and clubs for festivals, and received a Churchill Fellowship in 2010 to study outdoor theatre in Europe. Geoff has previously worked at Belvoir on *Diving for Pearls* and *Dance Camp*. He is currently the Resident Designer at State Theatre Company of South Australia. Geoff's awards include the Helpmann Award for Best Scenic Design for *Little Bird* (State Theatre Company), the Ruby Award for Sustained Contribution, a Green Room Award for Best Lighting Design for *Night Letters*, and a Sydney Theatre Award for Best Lighting Design for *Never Did Me Any Harm*.

Colin Friels

Renato Musolino

TOM CONROY Jimmy

Tom graduated from the Victorian College of the Arts in 2009. For Belvoir he has appeared in *Mother Courage and Her Children* and *Small and Tired*. His other theatre credits include *Cock* (Melbourne Theatre Company/ La Boite); *Spring Awakening* (Sydney Theatre Company); *romeo&juliet* (State Theatre Company of South Australia); *Moth* (Malthouse/Arena Theatre Company); *Romeo and Juliet* (Bell Shakespeare); *The Sweetest Thing* (B Sharp/Arts Radar); *When the Rain Stops Falling* (New Theatre); *Delectable Shelter* (The Hayloft Project); *Land & Sea* (Brink Productions); *The Share* (five.point.one); *Heaven* (Old 505); and *night maybe* (Stuck Pigs Squealing). In 2014 Tom was a dramaturgy intern for Playwriting Australia. He has worked on script developments for Belvoir, Playwriting Australia, Bell Shakespeare, Brink and Queensland Theatre Company. His screen work includes *Hamlet* for Bell Shakespeare/ABC Splash Content. Tom's performance in *Something Natural But Very Childish* (La Mama) garnered him a Green Room Award for Best Male Actor in Independent Theatre.

ROBERT COUSINS Set & Costume Designer

For Belvoir **Robert** has designed sets for *Seventeen*, *Mother Courage and Her Children*, *Oedipus Schmoedipus*, *Miss Julie*, *Cat on a Hot Tin Roof*, *Peter Pan*, *Conversation Piece*, *Strange Interlude*, *Babyteeth*, *Cloudstreet*, *Page 8*, *As You Like It*, *Twelfth Night*, *Aliwa*, *Waiting for Godot*, *The Threepenny Opera*, *Gulpilil*, *A Midsummer Night's Dream* and *Who's Afraid of Virginia Woolf?*. His other design credits include *Medea* (Toneelgroep, Amsterdam); *Der Ring Des Nibelungen* (Opera Australia); *Julius Caesar, The Season at Sarsaparilla, Art of War, The Serpent's Teeth, The War of the Roses, Pygmalion, Under Milk Wood* (Sydney Theatre Company); *Moving Target* (Malthouse Theatre); *Weather* (Lucy Guerin Inc); *The Eternity Man* (Almeida Theatre, London); *Shades of Gray* (Sydney Dance Company); and *Night Letters* (State Theatre Company of South Australia). His set and costumes credits include *Motion Picture* (Lucy Guerin Inc); *Kafka's Metamorphosis, Fat Pig* (Sydney Theatre Company); *This Show Is About People* (Shaun Parker); *House Among the Stars, The Merchant of Venice, Drowning in My Ocean of You* (State Theatre Company of South Australia); *The Dreamed Life* (Comeout01); and *The Duckshooter* (Brink Productions). For film, Robert was production designer for *Candy, Romulus My Father, Balibo* and *Ruben Guthrie*. Robert wrote and edited *25 Belvoir Street*, a history of the first 25 years of theatre at Belvoir.

OTIS JAI DHANJI Oliver / Alvaro (Sydney season)

Otis is 13 and thrilled to be making his professional theatre debut at Belvoir. He has been performing from an early age and loves anything to do with drama and dance. Otis is home-schooled and has appeared in the Homeschool Creative Arts drama production every year since the age of five. For the last two years Otis has had the lead male role. When not performing, Otis writes prolifically. He has written many short stories, a play and is determined to finish his first novel. He also loves making short films – either directing his brothers and friends or using stop-motion animation. Otis also enjoys playing soccer. He been doing Taekwondo for nine years and has a black belt.

CALIN DIAMOND Oliver / Alvaro (Adelaide season)

Calin was born in Cloquet, Minnesota, USA, in 2002 into a performing arts family, and literally grew up on different stages all over the world. At the age of three Calin performed his first magic trick to an audience of over 500. By the age of eight Calin had already attended many magic seminars and workshops and in 2009 had the rare opportunity to be on stage with one of his mentors, Lance Burton, at the Monte Carlo Resort and Casino in Las Vegas. In 2011 Calin was asked to perform at the IBM (International Brotherhood of Magicians) Convention in Dallas, Texas. In 2013 Calin performed his own stage show at the Adelaide Fringe. Later that year he performed in the Genting Highlands World Resorts, Malaysia. The highlight of his career was when Luis de Matos (Master Magician from The Illusionists 2.0) asked him to perform in Spain and Portugal in 2014.

NATE EDMONDSON Sound Designer

Nate is a graduate of NIDA's Production course. He was Sound Designer on Belvoir's productions of *Seventeen* in 2015 and *This Heaven* in 2013, Associate Sound Designer on *Kill The Messenger* in 2015, and Assistant Sound Designer on *Angels In America: Part 1 & 2* in 2013. Nate's other credits include *Romeo And Juliet* (STC); *Never Did Me Any Harm* [Associate Sound Designer] (Force Majeure/STC); *Once We Were* (Sydney Dance Company); *The Tempest, Romeo And Juliet, As You Like It* [Associate Sound Designer], *Macbeth, The Winter's Tale* (Bell Shakespeare); *A Riff On Keef: The Human Myth, MinusOneSister, Caress/Ache, The Witches, Music, Jump For Jordan, The Floating World* [Assistant Sound Designer], *Rust And Bone, This Year's Ashes* (Griffin Theatre Company); *Salomé, Lord Of The Flies* (Malthouse Helium); *Good Works, Daylight Saving, All My Sons, Torch Song Trilogy, The Greening Of Grace, The Seafarer, The Paris Letter, The Coming World* (Darlinghurst Theatre); *Fireface, The Hiding Place* (ATYP); *Shellshock* (Riverside Theatres); *When The Rain Stops Falling, The Temperamentals, Julius Caesar* (New Theatre); *Jack Kerouac's Essentials Of Spontaneous Prose, Lenny Bruce: 13 Daze Un-Dug In Sydney, Psycho Beach Party, Fallout, Wrecking, The Highway Crossing, Lyrebird, Pictures Of Bright Lights, Flightfall* (Rock Surfers); *Of Mice And Men* (Sport For Jove); *I Am My Own Wife, A Girl With Sun In Her Eyes, Freak Winds* (Red Line Productions); *Misterman* (Siren Theatre Company); *Decay, River* (Old 505); *The Very Hungry Caterpillar Show* (Michael Sieders Presents); *Departures* (Ken Unsworth/Australian Dance Artists); *The Light Box* (Unhappen/Fat Boy Dancing); *Two By Two* (Little Ones Theatre); *Scenes From An Execution, King Lear, Measure For Measure* (Tooth And Sinew); *Today We're Alive* (Wildie Creative Enterprises); *Fefu And Her Friends* (Red Rabbit Theatre); *Elektra, Medea, Phaedra* (AIM Dramatic Arts); *Away, Living With Lady Macbeth, If Only The Lonely Were Home* (Kambala School); *Alice In Wonderland* (NIDA Open Program); *Much Ado About Nothing* [Guest Sound Designer], *NIDA Gala* [2010 & 2012] (NIDA). Nate's short film and television work includes *Ten Little Rubber Ducks, I Am Not A Work Of Art, Disturbing Bodies* (ABC Fresh Blood), *The Light Box, Pretty, Gibney's Island, Kaleidoscope*.

Louisa Mignone

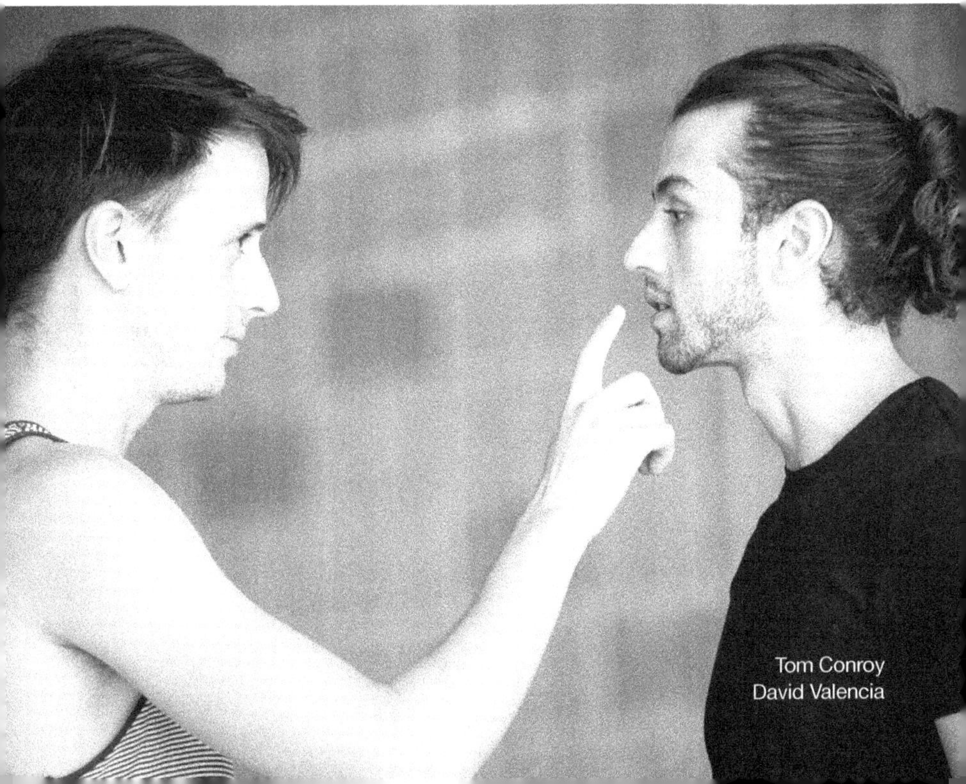

Tom Conroy
David Valencia

COLIN FRIELS Detective Grubbe / others

Colin's theatre credits include *Death of a Salesman* (Belvoir); *Red* (Melbourne Theatre Company); *Zebra, Victory, Copenhagen, The School for Scandal, Macbeth, The Temple* (Sydney Theatre Company); *Shadow and Splendour, The Cherry Orchard* (Royal Queensland Theatre Company); *The Incorruptible* (Playbox Theatre); *Cloud Nine, Miss Julie* and *The Bear* (Nimrod). Colin's television credits include *Jack Irish: Bad Debts, Wild Boys, Killing Time, Bastard Boys, Blackjack, Temptation, My Husband My Killer, The Farm, For the Term of His Natural Life* and *Water Rats*. His film credits include *The Eye of the Storm, A Heartbeat Away, Tomorrow When the War Began, Matching Jack, The Informant, The Nothing Men, Solo, The Book of Revelation, Tom White, The Man Who Sued God, Dark City, Mr Reliable, Cosi, Angel Baby, A Good Man in Africa, Dingo, High Tide, Malcolm, The Coolangatta Gold* and *Monkey Grip*. Colin received a Helpmann Award for Best Male Actor for *Copenhagen*, a TV Week Logie Award for Best Actor in *Water Rats*, an AFI Award for Best Actor in a Television Drama for *Water Rats*, and a Best Actor AFI Award for *Malcolm*. In 2016 Colin will be seen on stage again at Belvoir in *Faith Healer*, directed by Judy Davis.

MATT GOLDWYN Oliver / Alvaro (Adelaide season)

Matt is 12 years old and lives in the Adelaide Hills of South Australia. His acting and singing career began seriously in 2014, both locally and in the USA. He has since attended many coaching classes and a film camp in Los Angeles, as well as developing his acting in Adelaide. In addition to shooting *Pow Wow Night Wild* in LA, Matt has worked on local projects, while also writing and recording original music and songs. *Mortido* is Matt's stage debut.

LUKE McGETTIGAN Stage Manager

Luke is Belvoir's Resident Stage Manager. For Belvoir he has stage managed *Seventeen, Elektra / Orestes, Radiance, The Glass Menagerie, Brothers Wreck, Once in Royal David's City, Miss Julie, Forget Me Not, Peter Pan* (including New York tour), *Private Lives, Death of a Salesman, Babyteeth, Summer of the Seventeenth Doll, Neighbourhood Watch, The Wild Duck* (including UK and Europe tours), *Namatjira* (Belvoir/Big hART), *Page 8, The End, That Face, The Promise, Scorched, Antigone, Keating!, The Little Cherry Orchard* and *The Caucasian Chalk Circle*. His other credits include *The Pig Iron People, The Give and Take, Bed, La Dispute* (Sydney Theatre Company); *Like a Fishbone* (Sydney Theatre Company/Griffin Theatre Company); *The Government Inspector, The Tempest, The Servant of Two Masters, The Comedy of Errors, The Taming of the Shrew* (Bell Shakespeare); *Paradise City, Through the Wire* (Performing Lines); *Alive at Williamstown Pier* (Griffin Theatre Company); *Scam, Abroad With Two Men* (Christine Dunstan Productions); *Flexitime, Market Forces, Shoe Horn Sonata, Blinded by the Sun* (Ensemble Theatre); *The Complete Works of William Shakespeare* (Spirit Productions); *Twelfth Night, Arms and the Man, Much Ado About Nothing, Spring Awakening* (Railway Street Theatre Company); *Barmaids, Radiance* (New England Theatre Company); *My Girragundji* (Canute Productions); and *Dog Logs* (Marguerite Pepper Productions).

LOUISA MIGNONE Scarlet / Sybille

Louisa trained at Flinders Drama Centre, Adelaide. Her theatre credits include *The Boys* (Griffin Theatre Company); *Pork Stiletto* (The Old Fitz); *Fugitive, Boom Bah!* (Windmill Performing Arts); *Best We Forget, Make Me Honest Make Me Wedding Cake, That's His Style* (isthisyours?); and *Actors At Work* (Bell Shakespeare). Her television credits include *Miss Fisher's Murder Mysteries, Rake, Fat Tony & Co, Wonderland, East West 101, My Place* and *Danger 5*. Louisa has appeared in the films *Infini, Trust Fund, Two Fists One Heart*.

RENATO MUSOLINO Monte / Darren Shine

Renato is a graduate of Adelaide's Centre for the Performing Arts (now AC Arts). In 2003 he undertook a mentorship/observership at The Actors Studio in New York City. For the State Theatre Company of South Australia his credits include *Othello, The Seagull, The Comedy of Errors* (co-production with Bell Shakespeare), *The Kreutzer Sonata, In the Next Room (Or the Vibrator Play), Three Sisters, The Zoo Story, The Misanthrope, Blue Orange, Mnemonic* and *King Lear*. Renato's other credits include *Rust and Bone* (Griffin Theatre Company); *Amadeus* (Chopt Logic); *Romeo and Juliet* (Lightning Strike); *Danny and the Deep Blue Sea* (Natland Theatre); *Carboni* (Urbino, Italy, Canberra Multicultural Festival and Eureka Week, Ballarat); *What I Heard About Iraq, The Homecoming, Bash* (Holden Street Theatre); *Assassins, True West* (Flying Penguin Productions); *Helly's Magic Cup* (Windmill Performing Arts); *The Ballad of Pondlife McGurk* (Windmill Performing Arts/Catherine Wheels, Scotland); and *The Good Son*. Renato has appeared in the feature film *The Caterpillar Wish*, and on TV in *Plonk*. His ABC Radio National credits include *Clark in Sarajevo, The Ruby, The Death of Napoleon, Blood on My Hands, Clerk Ascending* and *Joshua's Book*.

SEAN PROUDE Assistant Stage Manager

Originally from country South Australia, **Sean** graduated from the Western Australian Academy of Performing Arts' Stage Management course in 2014. He has been assistant stage manager on *AIDA* (Handa Opera on Sydney Harbour) and Sydney Festival, and worked as a harbour production assistant on the New Year's Eve Festival. In 2014 Sean was seconded to *The Magic Flute* (Opera on the Beach) and *Madama Butterfly* (Handa Opera on Sydney Harbour).

Colin Friels

Tom Conroy
Renato Musolino

THE SWEATS Composer

THE SWEATS is Pete Goodwin, an award winning composer and sound designer for theatre, film, television and advertising. Pete has been the resident composer for RealTV since the company was formed in 2000, and has created scores for all their productions to date, including: *The Dark Room, Random, War Crimes, Hoods, Children of the Black Skirt, Chook, Do You Love Me?, The Orphanage Project, Kingswood Kids, Princess of Suburbia* and *The Suitcase*. He has also composed scores for the productions *Miss Julie, The Dark Room* (Belvoir); *Death and the Maiden* (Sydney Theatre Company/Melbourne Theatre Company); *Love and Information* (Sydney Theatre Company/Malthouse Theatre); *Meme Girls, The Good Person Of Szechuan* (including live on-stage performance) (Malthouse Theatre); *Buyer And Cellar, The Effect, Yellow Moon, Cock* (with Missy Higgins), *Constellations, Helicopter, Random* (Melbourne Theatre Company); *Tall Man, Status Update, Crossed* (La Mama); *The Fortunes Of Richard Mahony, A Conversation, The Orphanage Project, Black Comedy, The Real Inspector Hound, The Memory Of Water, Far Away* (Queensland Theatre Company); *The Motion Of Light In Water, Cock, and Kingswood Kids* (La Boite). THE SWEATS film and TV work includes *Drowning, She Loves Me She Loves Me Not, Stray, And Everything Nice, Transient* and *Booth* (Film) and *Saved* (TV). THE SWEATS is also a recording artist and DJ. Recordings include *You Make Me Feel EP* and *Samo EP*.

DAVID VALENCIA El Gallito

David is a graduate of the National Institute of Dramatic Art. His stage credits include *Blood Wedding* (Malthouse Theatre); *Blackrock* (Australian Theatre Company, Los Angeles); *The Criminals* (Old 505 Theatre); *Deviator* (PVI Collective); and *The Motherfucker with the Hat* (Aquila Morong Studio, Los Angeles). His other theatre credits include *Red, A Man for All Seasons, Cabaret, Twelfth Night, The Seagull, Noises Off!, Pictures of Bright Lights, Pains of Youth* and *Flight* for NIDA. In 2015 David headlined Elijah Wood's production of *The Boy* (2015 SXSW Film Festival, 2015 BFI London Film Festival, 48th Sitges Film Festival, 2015 Stanley Film Festival), as well as Latin-American indies *Bad Days* (2015 Warsaw International Film Festival) and *The Enforcers* (2015 Bogota International Film Festival).

JENNIFER WHITE Dialect Coach

Jennifer graduated from NIDA with a Post Graduate Diploma (Voice) and from UWS Nepean with a Bachelor of Arts (Acting). She is also a professional musical theatre/cabaret singer and voiceover artist, and teaches voice, dialects, Shakespeare and text at NIDA. For Sydney Theatre Company she was dialect coach on *Tot Mom* and *August: Osage County* (STC/Steppenwolf Theatre Company), and dialect consultant on *True West*. She was dialect coach on *Solomon & Marion* (Melbourne Theatre Company); *The Sea Project* (Griffin/Arthur Productions); and on 19 plays for Ensemble Theatre. Jennifer's film and television coaching includes *The Hunter, J. Edgar, The Water Diviner, Unbroken, The Outlaw Michael Howe, Bikie Wars* and the upcoming *Joe Cinque's Consolation*. She was dialect and foreign languages coach on the musicals *Chitty Chitty Bang Bang, West Side Story, Chicago, The Rocky Horror Show*, and Hayes Theatre Company's *Sweet Charity, Miracle City* and *Dogfight*. In 2015 Jennifer was the foreign languages coach for the Netball World Cup Opening Ceremony, where she coached an Australian choir in the pronunciation of the national anthems of Malawi, New Zealand, Samoa, Singapore, Sri Lanka, South Africa and Wales.

Tom Conroy
Colin Friels

Louisa Mignone
Renato Musolino

ANTHEA WILLIAMS Dramaturg

Anthea is Belvoir's Associate Director – Literary. For Belvoir she has directed *Kill the Messenger*, *Cinderella*, *Forget Me Not* and *Old Man* and has been dramaturg on a number of works including *Seventeen*, *Samson*, *This Heaven* and *Small and Tired*. Prior to joining Belvoir in 2011 Anthea was Associate Director bushfutures at London's Bush Theatre, where her directing credits include *Two Cigarettes*, *50 Ways to Leave Your Lover*, *50 Ways to Leave Your Lover at Christmas*, *Turf*, *suddenlossofdignity.com*, and the musical *The Great British Country Fete*. Anthea's work toured Britain extensively, including to The Drum Theatre Plymouth, The Ustinov Bath, The Tobacco Factory Bristol, the Norwich Playhouse, North Wall Arts Centre Cambridge and the Latitude Festival. Her other directing credits include *A Question* (nabokov); *The Real You* (SmackBang); and *Quiet* (Fontanel). Prior to working at the Bush Theatre, Anthea was the Co-Artistic Director of SmackBang Theatre Company and the producer of Massive Company, both in Auckland, New Zealand. Anthea trained at the Victorian College of the Arts (Directing) and the University of New South Wales.

SCOTT WITT Movement Director

Scott is an award-winning artist who has worked for 30 years as a writer/adaptor, fight director, movement consultant, actor, director and clown. As a fight director and/or movement consultant his theatre credits number well over 200 professional productions, including *Ivanov*, *Seventeen*, *Mother Courage and Her Children*, *Samson*, *Elektra / Orestes*, *Kill the Messenger*, *Radiance*, *A Christmas Carol*, *Hedda Gabler*, *Oedipus Schmoedipus*, *Miss Julie*, *Angels in America*, *Peter Pan*, *Beautiful One Day*, *Medea*, *Private Lives*, *Death of a Salesman*, *Babyteeth*, *The Dark Room*, *Summer of the Seventeenth Doll*, *Gwen in Purgatory*, *That Face* (Belvoir); *Suddenly Last Summer*, *After Dinner*, *Noises Off*, *Waiting for Godot*, *Rosencrantz & Guildenstern Are Dead*, *The Fury*, *Secret River*, *Mariage Blanc*, *Signs of Life*, *Les Liaisons Dangereuses*, *Zebra*, *God of Carnage*, *True West*, *A Streetcar Named Desire*, *The Wonderful World of Dissocia* (Sydney Theatre Company); *The Tempest*, *As You Like It*, *Tartuffe*, *Henry V*, *Comedy of Errors*, *Henry IV*, *The Taming of the Shrew* (Bell Shakespeare); *Monkey* (Theatre of Image), *Death and the Maiden*, *Private Lives*, (Melbourne Theatre Company); *Cyrano*, *Othello*, *Comedy of Errors*, *Hamlet* (Sport for Jove); *Rabbits*, *Faust*, *Rigoletto*, *Macbeth*, *Don Giovanni* (Opera Australia); *Anatomy Titus: Fall of Rome*, *The Alchemist*, *Richard III* (Bell Shakespeare/Queensland Theatre Company); *Macbeth*, *Toy Symphony*, *The Crucible*, *School of Arts*, *Stones in His Pockets*, *Who's Afraid of Virginia Woolf?*, *The Glass Menagerie*, *Private Lives* (Queensland Theatre Company). Scott has been a proud member of MEAA since 1988, is the current Artistic Director of the International Order of the Sword & the Pen, and is the Lecturer in Movement at the National Institute of Dramatic Art.

STATE THEATRE COMPANY
of South Australia

2016

Season Tickets On Sale Now!

STATETHEATRECOMPANY.COM.AU

BELVOIR

JASPER JONES
2 JAN – 7 FEB

THE BLIND GIANT IS DANCING
13 FEB – 20 MAR

THE GREAT FIRE
2 APR – 8 MAY

THE EVENTS
12 MAY – 12 JUN

BACK AT THE DOJO
18 JUN – 17 JUL

TWELFTH NIGHT
23 JUL – 4 SEP

THE DROVER'S WIFE
17 SEP – 16 OCT

FAITH HEALER
22 OCT – 27 NOV

GIRL ASLEEP
2 – 24 DEC

THE TRIBE
19 JAN – 7 FEB

HANNAH GADSBY – DOGMATIC
20 – 22 MAY

RUBY'S WISH
21 SEP – 9 OCT

TITLE AND DEED
13 OCT – 6 NOV

2016 SEASON

**COME AND SEE
SUBSCRIBE NOW
BELVOIR.COM.AU**

Belvoir Staff

18 Belvoir Street, Surry Hills NSW 2010
Email mail@belvoir.com.au Web belvoir.com.au
Administration (02) 9698 3344 Facsimile (02) 9319 3165 Box Office (02) 9699 3444

Artistic Director
Eamon Flack
Executive Director
Brenna Hobson
Deputy Executive Director & Head of Development
Nathan Bennett

Belvoir Board
Anne Britton
Mitchell Butel
Andrew Cameron (Chair)
Luke Carroll
Tracey Driver
Richard Evans
Eamon Flack
Brenna Hobson
Ian Learmonth
Olivia Pascoe
Peter Wilson

Belvoir St Theatre Board
Trefor Clayton (Chair)
Stuart McCreery
Angela Pearman
Nick Schlieper
Kingsley Slipper

Artistic & Programming
Associate Producer
Luke Cowling
Associate Director – Literary
Anthea Williams

Education
Education Manager
Jane May
Acting Education Coordinator
Hannah McBride

Administration
Artistic Administrator
John Woodland
Trainee Administration Coordinator
Anthony Blanch

Finance & Operations
Head of Finance & Operations
Kate Chalker
Acting Company Accountant
Jonathan Phillips
Accounts Administrator
Susan Jack
IT & Operations Manager
Jan S. Goldfeder

Box Office
Box Office Manager
Tanya Ginori-Cairns
Assistant Box Office Managers
Andrew Dillon
Laura Henderson
Subscriptions Manager
Jason Lee

Front of House
Front of House Manager
Ohmeed Ahi
Assistant Front of House Manager
Scott Pirlo

Development
Philanthropy Manager
Liz Tomkinson
Development Coordinator
Aimee Timmins

Marketing
Marketing Manager
Amy Goodhew
Digital Content Producer
Marty Jamieson
Publications Manager
Gabrielle Bonney
Publicity & Public Affairs Manager
Elly Michelle Clough

Production
Head of Production
Warren Sutton
Production Coordinator
Eliza Maunsell
Technical Manager
Will Jacobs
Resident Stage Manager
Luke McGettigan
Staging & Construction Manager
Penny Angrick
Staging & Construction Assistant
Brianna Russell
Costume Coordinator
Judy Tanner
Senior Technician
Caitlin Porter

About State Theatre Company

State Theatre Company of South Australia is the state's flagship professional theatre company performing an annual season of classic and contemporary Australian and international theatre works at its main performance home – the Dunstan Playhouse. The Company is a major community and cultural resource for all South Australians and is vital to artistic life in the state.

State Theatre Company also plays an important role in the bigger picture of the Australian theatre scene, contributing touring productions and providing employment and career opportunities for artists and technical and administrative staff. We are committed to the development of new works for the stage and to the development of South Australian artists through our creative fellowship programs.

Staff

BOARD MEMBERS
John Irving (Chair), Terence Crawford, Jodi Glass, Kristen Greber, Christine Guille, Justin Jamieson, Hon. Anne Levy AO, Jodie Newton

FOUNDATION BOARD MEMBERS
Malcolm Gray (Chair), Peter deCure, Kristen Greber, Christine Guille, Tony Keenan, Diané Ranck, Loretta Reynolds, Meredyth Sarah AM, Alison Smallacombe, Andrew Sweet

EXECUTIVE DIRECTOR/PRODUCER
Rob Brookman

ARTISTIC DIRECTOR
Geordie Brookman

RESIDENT DIRECTOR
Nescha Jelk

RESIDENT DESIGNER
Geoff Cobham

ARTISTIC PROGRAM MANAGER
Shelley Lush

ARTISTIC COUNSEL*
Julian Meyrick

MARKETING MANAGER
Kristy Rebbeck

MARKETING COORDINATOR
Tara McHenry

PUBLIC RELATIONS COORDINATOR
Lindsay Ferris

GRAPHIC DESIGN & DIGITAL CONTENT COORDINATOR
Robin Mather

MARKETING ASSISTANT
Ben Allison

DEVELOPMENT MANAGER
Guy Ross

PHILANTHROPY COORDINATOR
Bernadette Woods

EVENTS & CORPORATE PARTNERSHIPS COORDINATOR
Kimberley Martin

EDUCATION MANAGER
Robyn Brookes

FINANCE MANAGER
Natalie Loveridge

ADMINISTRATION COORDINATOR
Fiona Lukac

PRODUCTION MANAGER
Gavin Norris

PRODUCTION & FINANCE COORDINATOR
Bronwyn Pelmer

PROPS COORDINATOR
Stuart Crane

PRODUCTION STAGE MANAGER
Melanie Selwood

WORKSHOP SUPERVISOR
John Meyer

LEADING HAND
Areste Nicola

CARPENTER & PROP MAKER
Patrick Duggin

CARPENTER & METALWORKER
Guy Botroff

CARPENTER
Michael Ambler

PROPS ASSISTANT
Kyle Bowen

HEAD ELECTRICIAN
Sue Grey-Gardner

SCENIC ART
Sandra Anderson

PROP SHOP
Robin Balogh

HEAD OF WARDROBE
Kellie Jones

WARDROBE PRODUCTION SUPERVISOR
Enken Haage

COSTUME TECHNICIAN
Martine Micklem

HAIR, MAKE-UP, WIGS & COSTUME HIRE
Jana DeBiasi

OVERSEAS REPRESENTATIVES (LONDON)
Yolanda Bird & Diana Franklin

OVERSEAS REPRESENTATIVE (NEW YORK)
Stuart Thompson

*Julian Meyrick's services are provided courtesy of Flinders University

State Theatre Company Donors

State Theatre Company gratefully acknowledges its Foundation patron Maureen Ritchie and all donors who have contributed gifts in the past year. State Theatre Company of South Australia is a tax deductible fund listed on the Register of Cultural Organisations under Subdivision 30-B of the Income Tax Assessment Act 1997. Donations of $2 or more are tax deductible.

$10,000+
Dr Neal Blewett AC
Alison & David Smallacombe (Supporting State R&D)
Diané Ranck
Kim Williams AM
Hill Smith Gallery

$5,000+
Arts Projects Australia
Rob Brookman AM & Verity Laughton
Ian Darling AM
Granger Charitable Trust
Malcolm Gray
Sonia Laidlaw (Supporting State R&D)
Pamela & David McKee
Pamela & Peter McKee
Loretta Reynolds
Maureen Ritchie
Roger Salkeld & Helen Bell

$2,000+
Biggs Charitable Trust
Jodi Glass & Adrian Tisato
Hancock Charitable Trust
Christine & Lorin Jenner
Hon Diana Laidlaw AM
Nicholas Linke
Dr Alex Markou
Judy Potter
Meredyth Sarah AM & Don Sarah AM
Dr Adam Sheridan
Merry Wickes
Silvana Zerella

$1,000+
Geordie Brookman & Nicki Bloom
Gustie & Tony deMaaijer
Mary Camilleri
Prof. John Chalmers AC
CMV Foundation
Rob & Jenny Creasey
Legh Davis
Jane & Ian Doyle
Ginger Fitzpatrick
Casandra Francas
Diana Fry
Chris Guille
Christine Guille
Alister Haigh
Dr Zen & Susie Herzberg
Amanda Horne
John Irving
Justin Jamieson
Hon. Anne Levy AO
Chester Osborne
Michael Madigan
Dr Jane & Dr Trevor Mudge
Jenni Mumford
Mary Parry
Libby Raupach OAM
Dr Nigel Steele Scott
Pat & Hugh Stretton AC
Sue Tweddell
Darren Mark Wright

$250+
Aldridge Family Endowment
Ben Allen
Hon. John Bannon AO
Lauryn Barrie
John Bishop AO
Imelda Blackwell
Hon. David & Elizabeth Bleby
Torben & Richelle Brookman
Graham Brookman
Clive & Jane Brooks
Robert Bryce & Lyn Edwards
Sharon Evans
Jacke & Paul Cammell
Sally Chapman
David & Annabelle Chan
Leonie Clyne
Peter Coad
Anthony & Caroline Davies
John & Judi Denton
Alex Diamantis
Peter Dobson
Kay Dowling
Professor Anne Edwards AO
Joy Fletcher
Dr Kristine Gebbie
Steve Geddes & Dr Elaine Pretorius
Donald George
Mark Goddard
Dr Peter Goldsworthy AM
Sue Grediey
Joanne Griffiths
John & Rosemary Gumley
Peter & Elizabeth Hambly
Janet Hayes
Rhys & Vyvyan Horwood
Hon. Chris Harford AO
Sam Jackman
Glenys Jones OAM
John Kirkwood
Sue Kitchener
Maureen Lawlor
Joan Lea
June Letton
Roland Lever & Stephanie Thorpe
Tony Llewellyn-Jones
Virginia Lynch
Greg Mackie OAM
Professor Richard Maltby
Des Marnane
Jean Matthews
Teena Munn
Kenneth O'Brien
John Ovenden
Bernie Pfitzner
Dr George Potter
Julie Redman
Suzie Riley
Professor Ian & Professor Kaye Roberts-Thomson
Mick Roche
Guy Ross & Ellen Poyner
Kate Russell
Richard Ryan AO
Jodie & Mark Saturno
John Schulze
Tony Seymour
Kenneth Shepherd
Anne Skipper AM
Colette Smith
Tracey Spear
Christopher Stone
Jenny & Sarah Strathearn
Tania Salan
Lisa Temple
Karen Thomas
Marika Tiggemann
Helen Tiller
Fiona Tillmann
Diana Vickery
Brian & Jane Ward
Ann Wells
Patrick Wells
Julie Williams
Judy White

GOLD SUBSCRIBERS
Imelda Blackwell
Rob & Jenny Creasey
Gustie & Tony deMaaijer
Kay Dowling
Robert Bryce & Lyn Edwards
Kath Ferguson
John & Rosemary Gumley
Malcolm Gray & Laura Healy
Sam & Margo Hill-Smith
Hon. Anne Levy AO
Des Marnane
Dr Jane & Dr Trevor Mudge
James Ninham
Sarah Paddick
Steve Geddes & Dr Elaine Pretorius
Diane Ranck
John & Jeanette Reynolds
Loretta Reynolds & Michael Tienemann
Roger Salkeld & Helen Bell
David & Alison Smallacombe
Jenny & Sarah Strathearn
Rob Brady & Bridget Walters
Silvana Zerella

State Theatre Company Donors

For information about how you might make a positive contribution to the ongoing growth and achievements of State Theatre Company, please contact Guy Ross, Development Manager on 8415 5308 or guy@statetheatrecompany.com.au

JILL BLEWETT PLAYWRIGHTS AWARD FUND
This prestigious Award, established in memory of Company Chair Jill Blewett, is granted biennially and includes a full commission to the winner, along with a week-long creative development.

Thyne Reid Foundation
Hon. Dr Neal Blewett AC
Kim Williams AM
Rob Brookman AM & Verity Laughton
Malcolm Gray
Pat & Hugh Stretton AC
Prof. John Chalmers AC
Hon. Anne Levy AO
Hon. Chris Hurford AO
Alex Diamantis
Hon. John Bannon AO
Megan Stoyles
Leonie Scrivener
Trevor & Jane Wilson
Tony Llewellyn-Jones
Guy Ross & Ellen Poyner

CREATIVE DEVELOPMENT DONOR CIRCLE
Providing valuable philanthropic support for the ongoing artistic achievements of State Theatre Company through the creative development of new Australian work.

David & Alison Smallacombe - Ambassadors
Arts Projects Australia
Rob Brookman AM & Verity Laughton
Jane Doyle
Jodi Glass
Malcolm Gray
Chris Guille
Alister Haigh
Margo & Sam Hill-Smith
John Irving
Chester Osborne
Judy Potter
Libby Raupach OAM
Roger Salkeld & Helen Bell
Don Sarah AM
Merry Wickes

EDUCATION PROGRAM DONOR CIRCLE
Providing valuable philanthropic support in nurturing the next generation of artists and audiences across South Australia.

Diané Ranck - Ambassador
Amanda Horne
Meredyth Sarah AM
Christine & Lorin Jenner
Silvana Zerella

DRAMATIC WOMEN
Providing philanthropic support for Summer of the Seventeenth Doll

Sally Chapman
Jane Doyle
Professor Anne Edwards AO
Casandra Francas
Christine Guille
Janet Hayes
Christine Jenner
Glenys Jones OAM
Sue Kitchener
Virginia Lynch
Pamela McKee
Bernie Pfitzner
Diané Ranck
Julie Redman
Meredyth Sarah AM
Alison Smallacombe
Tracey Spear
Tania Salan
Lisa Temple
Karen Thomas
Marika Tiggemann
Helen Tiller
Fiona Tillmann
Sue Tweddell
Julie Williams

We also acknowledge all 175 of our donors who have kindly made contributions below $250

State Theatre Company acknowledges the passing of Hugh Stretton AC

Belvoir Donors

We give our heartfelt thanks to all our donors for their loyal and generous support.

Creative Development Fund

$10,000+
Andrew Cameron AM & Cathy Cameron
Sherry-Hogan Foundation
Kim Williams AM & Catherine Dovey

$5,000 – $9,999
Anonymous (1)
Stephen Allen
Anne Britton
Hartley Cook
Gail Hambly
Louise Herron & Clark Butler
Peter & Rosemary Ingle
Helen Lynch AM & Helen Bauer
Frank Macindoe
Victoria Taylor

$2,000 – $4,999
Neil Armfield AO
Jill & Richard Berry
Justin Butterworth
& Stephen Asher
John Cary
Janet & Trefor Clayton
Michael Coleman
Victoria Holthouse
David Marr
David Robb

$500 – $1,999
Helen Argiris
Richard Banks
Chris Collett
Joanna Collins
Linda English
Timothy Hale
Roey Higgs
Stephanie Hutchinson
Angus Hutchinson
Alec Leopold
Janine Perrett
Penelope Seidler
Alenka Tindale
Sheryl Weil

Co-Conspirators

$10,000+
Gail Hambly
Anita Jacoby
Mark Warburton
Peter Wilson
Cathy Yuncken

The Chair's Group

$3,000+
Judge Joe Harman
Marion Heathcote
& Brian Burfitt
Penny Ward
David & Jennifer Watson

$1,000 – $2,999
Antoinette Albert
Jill & Richard Berry
Jillian Broadbent AO
Chris Brown
Jan Chapman
& Stephen O'Rourke
Louise Christie
Wesley Enoch
Kathleen & Danny Gilbert
Sophie Guest
Michael Hobbs
Emma Hogan
Hilary Linstead
Ross McLean & Fiona Beith
Cajetan Mula (Honorary Member)
Steve & Belinda Rankine
Alex Oonagh Redmond
Michael Rose
& Jo D'Antonio
Ann Sherry AO
Kim Williams AM

2015 B Keepers

$5,000+
Robert & Libby Albert
Ellen Borda
Constructability Recruitment
Marion Heathcote & Brian Burfitt
Don & Leslie Parsonage

$3,000 – $4,999
Anonymous (1)
Bev & Phil Birnbaum
Anne Britton
Louise Christie
Suzanne & Michael Daniel
Colleen Kane
S Khouri & D Cross
Chantal & Greg Roger
Peter & Jan Shuttleworth

$2,000 – $2,999
Claire Armstrong
& John Sharpe
Dr Brian T. Carey
Chris & Bob Ernst
Cary & Rob Gillespie
Peter Graves
David & Kathryn Groves
David Haertsch
John Head
Jennifer Ledgar & Bob Lim
Louise Mitchell & Peter Pether
A Maxwell & R Godlee
Dr David Nguyen
Timothy & Eva Pascoe
Merilyn Sleigh &
Raoul de Ferranti
Judy Thomson
Lynne Watkins & Nicholas Harding

$1,000 – $1,999
Anonymous (3)
Berg Family Foundation
Max Bonnell
Dr Catherine Brown-Watt
Jan Burnswoods
Mary Jo & Lloyd Capps
Elaine Chia
Jane Christensen
Tracey Driver
Jeanne Eve
Wendy & Andrew Hamlin
Libby Higgin
Michael Hobbs
Avril Jeans
Kevin & Rosemarie
Jeffers-Palmer
Corinne & Rob Johnston
Margaret Johnston
A. le Marchant
Stephanie Lee
Atul Lele
Professor Elizabeth More AM
Jane Munro
K Nomchong SC
Jacqueline & Michael Palmer
Dr Natalie Pelham
Greeba Pritchard
David & Jill Pumphrey
Richard & Heather Rasker
Colleen Roche
Lesley & Andrew Rosenberg
Andrew & Louise Sharpe
Vivienne Sharpe
Jennifer Smith
Chris & Bea Sochan
Jeremy Storer & Annabel Crabb
Sue Thomson
Lisa Hamilton & Rob White
Paul & Jennifer Winch
Ian & Judy Wyatt

The Hive

$2,500
Anthony Baxter & Elly Michelle Clough
Nathan Bennett & Yael Perry
Justin Butterworth & Stephen Asher
Dan & Emma Chesterman
Este Darin-Cooper & Chris Burgess
Joanna Davidson & Julian Leeser
Tracey Driver
Ruth Higgins
Emma Hogan & Kim Hogan
Nicola Marcus
& Jeremy Goldschmidt
Bruce Meagher & Greg Waters
G W Outram & F E Holyoake
Olivia Pascoe
Andrew & Louise Sharpe
Simpsons Solicitors
Michael Sirmai

The Sky Foundation
Peter Wilson & James Emmett

Education Donors

$10,000+
Doc Ross Family Foundation
Susie & Nick Kelly
Ian Learmonth & Julia Pincus

$2,000 – $4,999
Anonymous (1)
Andrew Cameron AM
& Cathy Cameron
Estate of the late Angelo Comino
Matthew Hall
Julie Hannaford
Judge Joe Harman
Matthew Kidman
Olivia Pascoe

$500 – $1,999
Anonymous (6)
Len & Nita Armfield
Ian Barnett
Victor Baskir
David Bennett AO & Anne Bennett
Paul Bide
AB
Michael & Colleen Chesterman
Tracey Clancy
Karen Cooper & Simon Tuxen
Tim & Bryony Cox
Erin Devery
John B Fairfax AO & Libby Fairfax
JoAnna Fisher
Geoffrey & Patricia Gemmell
Dorothy Hoddinott AO
Sue Hyde
Peter & Rosemary Ingle
Stewart & Jillian Kellie

Ruth Layton
Jennifer Ledgar & Bob Lim
Mary Miltenyi
Ateka & Ted Ringrose
Peter & Janet Shuttleworth
Chris & Bea Sochan
Jeremy Storer & Annabel Crabb
Kerry Stubbs
Drew Tait
Carolyn Wright
Jason Yetton & Joanne Lam

General Donors

$10,000+
Anonymous (1)
Andrew Cameron AM
& Cathy Cameron
Ross Littlewood
& Alexandra Curtin
Helen Lynch AM & Helen Bauer

$2,000 – $4,999
Anonymous (2)
Baiba Berzins
Brenna Hobson
Anita Jacoby
Patricia Novikoff

$500 – $1,999
Anonymous (5)
Charles & Hannah Alexander
Ian Barnett
Victor Baskir
Christine Bishop
Ian Breden & Josephine Key
Dr & Mrs Gil Burton
Susan Casali
Michael & Colleen Chesterman
Lucy Chipkin

Tim & Bryony Cox
Jane Diamond
Diane Dunlop
Elizabeth Fairfax
Jono Gavin
Peter Gray & Helen Thwaites
Priscilla Guest
Kim Harding & Irene Miller
Harrison & Kate Higgs
Dorothy Hoddinott AO
David Jonas & Desmon Du Plessis
Iphygenia Kallinikos
Robert Kidd
Daniel Knight
Wolf Krueger & José Gutierrez
Frans Lauenstein
Sarah Lawrence
R S McColl
Anthony Nugent
Judy & Geoff Patterson
Kathirasen Ponnusamy
Angela Raymond
Leigh Sanderson
Abhijit & Janice Sengupta
Dr Agnes Sinclair
Eileen Slarke & Family
Andrew Smyth-Kirk
Dr Titia Sprague
Paul Stein
Harvey Stockwell
Mike Thompson
Suzanne & Ross Tzannes AM
Jane Uebergang
Chris Vik and Chelsea Albert
Sarah Walters
Louisa Ward & Tim Coen
Lynne Watkins & Nicholas Harding
Elizabeth Webby AM
Brian & Trish Wright

Belvoir is very grateful to accept all donations. Donations over $2 are tax deductible. If you would like to make a donation or would like further information about any of our donor programs please call our Development Team on 02 9698 3344 or email development@belvoir.com.au

List correct at time of printing.

Special Thanks
We would like to acknowledge Cajetan Mula, Len Armfield, Geoffrey Scharer and Jann Kohlman. They will always be remembered for their generosity to Belvoir.

These people and foundations supported the redevelopment of Belvoir Street Theatre and purchase of our warehouse.
Andrew & Cathy Cameron (refurbishment of theatre & warehouse)
Russell Crowe (Downstairs Theatre & purchase of warehouse)
The Gonski Foundation & The Nelson Meers Foundation (Gonski Meers Foyer)
Andrew & Wendy Hamlin (Brenna's office)
Hal Herron (The Hal Bar)
Geoffrey Rush (redevelopment of theatre)
Fred Street AM (Upstairs Dressing Room)

playwriting australia

MORE.
BETTER.
DIFFERENT.
AUSTRALIAN
PLAYS.

Jesse Butler in Albert Belz's Astroman, National Play Festival 2015. Photo: Shane Reid.

www.pwa.org.au

Luke Nguyen · Silvia Colloca · Adam Liaw · Shane Delia · Poh Ling Yeow

Thursday nights
sbs.com.au/food

SBSONE

The best of Sydney in one small email.

Be the first to know what's happening. Sign up for free at:
www.au.timeout.com/sydney/newsletter ▶

TimeOut Sydney

MOVIDA SYDNEY

BELVOIR DINING PARTNER

50 HOLT STREET
SURRY HILLS
TUES - SAT - 12PM - LATE

FOR PRE/POST THEATRE
BOOKINGS PLEASE CALL
OUR RESERVATIONS TEAM:
(02) 8964 7642.
OFFICE HOURS:
TUES - FRI 10AM-6PM
SAT 11AM-3PM

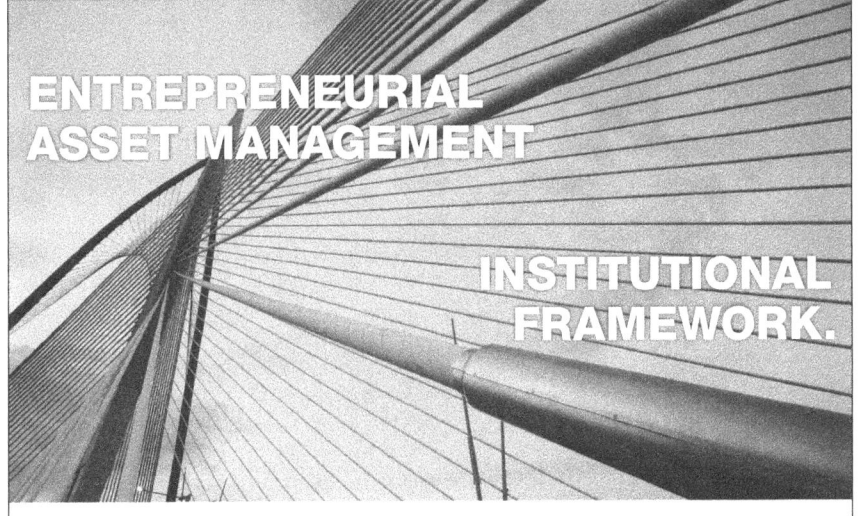

State Theatre Company Sponsors

GOVERNMENT PARTNERS

State Theatre Company of SA is assisted by the Australian Government through the Australia Council, its arts funding and advisory body.

PRESENTING PARTNERS

SUMMER OF THE SEVENTEENTH DOLL

THE POPULAR MECHANICALS

UNIVERSITY PARTNER

MEDIA PARTNERS

ASSOCIATE PARTNERS

TRUSTS & FOUNDATIONS

CORPORATE PARTNERS

 THOMSON GEER

SUPPORTING SPONSORS

TBar Tea Salon
American Chamber of Commerce in Australia
Flowers of Adelaide
Des's Cabs
Sphere Garden Design

CREATIVE PARTNERS

Belvoir Sponsors

Media Partners

Major Sponsors

IT Partner

Associate Sponsors

Key Supporter

 Indigenous Theatre at Belvoir supported by The Balnaves Foundation

Touring Fund

Mark Carnegie and Jessica Block

Event Sponsors

  the devonshire Coopers

MoVida HUNTER VALLEY Stays Mama's BUOI CELLARMASTERS

Government Partners

Youth & Education Supporters

Actors College Man

Trusts & Foundations

Copyright Agency Ltd
Coca-Cola Australia Foundation
Crown Resorts Foundation
Gandevia Foundation
The Greatorex Foundation
Teen Spirit Charitable Foundation
Vincent Fairfax Family Foundation

Supporters

Picket Studio
Thomas Creative
Time Out Australia

For more information on partnership opportunities please contact our Development team on 02 9698 3344 or development@belvoir.com.au

www.ingramcontent.com/pod-product-compliance
Lightning Source LLC
Chambersburg PA
CBHW050016090426
42734CB00021B/3290